NORWICH
AND THE
BROADS

1 Norwich Cathedral: the West Front

NORWICH
and
THE BROADS

J. Wentworth Day

London
B. T. BATSFORD LTD

First published, 1953

MADE AND PRINTED IN GREAT BRITAIN
BY JARROLD AND SONS LTD., LONDON AND NORWICH
FOR THE PUBLISHERS
B. T. BATSFORD LTD
4 FITZHARDINGE STREET, PORTMAN SQUARE, LONDON, W.1

PREFACE

IT is easy to become lyrical about a county you love. The temptation with Norfolk and especially with Norwich, its capital city, is to overpaint the picture. The colours are there. The lights illumine. The background is dimly magnificent. The foreground is sheer beauty and the middle distances are clear and mainly unspoiled. There you have the elements of a great picture.

But the Norfolk mind is suspicious of over-much praise. It is a factual, down-to-earth mind which, although it nurtures a fierce local pride, an immense self-sufficiency, is chary of soft words.

In this picture of Norwich and The Broads, I have tried to give some sense of the breadth and colour, some echo of the mighty past and some vision of the largely unspoiled present, which make up the East Norfolk picture. It is a unique corner of England with an atmosphere entirely its own. That is why it attracts tens of thousands of visitors from the corners of Britain. Here and there the holiday crowds, or some few who provide for them, have sullied the scene. Those exceptions are rare.

On the whole, despite their annual summer invasion, Norwich and The Broads remain supremely beautiful, coolly conscious of the space and dignity of ancient buildings, of wide green marshes, shining waters and noble sky-scapes which make the Broadland picture. Whether the threatened creation of a National Park will enhance or improve the scene is, to my mind, doubtful. I do not believe in the dead hand of remote bureaucratic control. Those who dwell in and by the English countryside are the best guardians thereof.

In the preparation of this book I have been helped by many good and old friends, dwellers in that ancient and lovable county. Chiefly among them were, or are, the late Lord Desborough; his head keeper, the late Jim Vincent; Mr. Roland Green, the celebrated bird artist of Hickling; Mr. Alan Savory of Brundall, who writes of his native marshes with the pen of a poet; Mr. Clifford Borrer, the eminent ornithologist; Mr. H. F. Brooker, General Manager of Blakes (Norfolk Broads Holidays) Ltd., and many

7

friends among the farmers and wildfowlers of Broadland, first and foremost of whom was that splendid naturalist and true son of the marshes, the late Arthur Patterson of Great Yarmouth. His charm⁄ing books are a lasting memorial to one who gave his whole life to the study and love of the Broads, their birds, fish, flowers and changing scenery.

Broadland is a unique and an irreplaceable echo of the older England. May it remain part of the soul and spirit of Norfolk rather than become, as indeed it may, a mere pawn of Whitehall Land Nationalisers.

J. Wentworth Day

CONTENTS

ACKNOWLEDGMENT

The Author and the Publishers wish to thank the following photographers whose work is represented in this book:

AEROFILMS LTD., for fig. 32

J. M. AIRD, for fig. 27

HALLAM ASHLEY, F.R.P.S., for figs. 2, 8, 18, 19, 21, 23, 24, 31, 39 and 55

A. E. COE AND SONS LTD., for figs. 9, 22, 36, 37, 41 and 47

LIONEL E. DAY, F.R.P.S., for figs. 12, 13 and 40

LEONARD and MARJORIE GAYTON, for figs. 4, 5 and 43

F. A. GIRLING, for fig. 38

ERIC J. HOSKING, F.R.P.S., for figs. 49–51 and 54

FORD JENKINS, for fig. 28

A. F. KERSTING, F.R.P.S., for figs. 1, 16, 20 and 30

THE MUSTOGRAPH AGENCY, for figs. 3, 7, 11, 26, 33–35, 44, 45, 52 and 56

PICTURE POST LIBRARY, for fig. 17

ALAN SAVORY, for figs. 42 and 53

IAN M. THOMSON, for fig. 48

They are also indebted to Mrs. Esmond Morse for her permission to reproduce fig. 15 from a photograph supplied by the Trustees of the Victoria and Albert Museum.

LIST OF ILLUSTRATIONS

Figure

2 The Yare Valley Marshes, near Postwick, Norfolk

3 A Norfolk Inn, with a chain ferry across the River Yare at Reedham

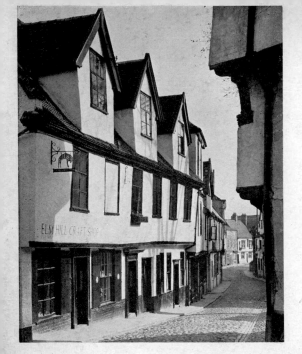

4 Elm Hill: sixteenth-century houses with Georgian windows

5 Sixteenth-century houses in the Close

NORWICH HOUSES

INTRODUCTION

ALMOST one might write of Norwich in the words of John Donne, that Elizabethan master of musical words, that it is a place

... where the dust of dead kings is blown into the street and the dust of the street blown into the river and the muddy river tumbles into the sea.

For there, indeed, is a proud and ancient city, tomb of prelates and mother of painters, city of commerce and riches, a place of soaring spires and red, huddled roofs, born from a bosom of green fields and shining rivers. It has, this ancient and lively city, a strange, proud spirit of its own, a spirit blent of the downright Norfolk mind which is all independence and hard work and thrift and shrewdness at a bargain, with a sort of underlying contempt of London and the soft and cunning ways of the South.

From that amalgam of hard, keen qualities, you might expect a hard, keen people, with little soul for beauty, no time for the past and no plan for the future, except a plan to make more money, to build more factories, to set a dreary, belching Manchester amid the green marshes and mustard-yellow uplands of the Norfolk scene where lucent rivers lace the landscape of Crome and Cotman with unpolluted silver.

There is, thank God, little or none of this unlovely quality of mind of "the stone-ribbed North" in the capital city of East Anglia. Modernism is there. Money is there. Great industries flourish. New red suburbs spread outwards. In all the ancientry there is no spirit of decay. The past in Norwich is the mother of the present and an inspiration for the future.

In this city of cattle and mustard, of shoe factories and steel works, there is a theatre unique in England, a School of Painters that is utterly English of the English, a museum of art and ornithology without a rival out of London. There is a cathedral of breathtaking beauty. There is a castle dominating it all which bore of old the haunting name of Blanchtower, and, at its feet, are streets and alleys and courts of medieval peace, cloisters of the centuries. And,

15

beyond the bounds of the city, lie the flat, green miles, the shining waters, the marching lines of witch-haired willows and the slow, broad rivers which make the beauty and mystery that is Broadland.

For there is the last primeval corner of the older England of marsh and fen, the England that has never known the thrust of a plough-share. The England of sighing reeds and secret meres, of the bittern booming ghostly in indigo nights of spring, of wild geese high and magical under winter stars, the heron fishing like a grey ghost in ancient jungles of reed and eel. We have lost the Fens that sheltered St. Guthlac and Hereward, the Fens that Kingsley loved. The great shining meres of Whittlesey and Soham, of Ugg and Trundle and Stretham are now mere flat, black fields, rich and unlovely, the kingdom of the potato. The Broads remain.

Here, in Eastern Norfolk, within the bounds of the ancient principality of the Bishops of Norwich who used to sit in the House of Lords under the proud title of Abbots of St. Benet-at-Holm, are marsh and mere, sighing reed-beds and tussocky level, where peewits wail and redshank spring on dancing wing. The beauty and the mystery endure. The last precious whisper of the ancient England of reed and fen and shining water has been caught and held. Through those misty levels, whose beauty changes through all colours of the painter's palette from spring to winter, flow slow and reedy rivers.

> Like some grave mighty thought threading a dream,
> And times and things, as in that vision, seem
> Keeping along it their eternal stands.

It is a pity irredeemable that George Borrow, dwelling in his gaunt house under the moaning firs on the reedy shores of Oulton Broad, roaring his Romany songs to the marshland stars, writing of Spain and Wild Wales and the wind on Mousehold Heath, did not write more of what lay at his door. For there was all beauty and all wildness. There was the ancient music of wind in the willows and the lift of a bird above shining waters. There was the tumbled glory of autumn reeds and marshland grasses in a flame of gold and fire-yellow and burnt umber over all the wild levels that ran into the west to the flare of incredible sunsets and into the east to the shining horizon of the sea. And always the sharp smell of the sea on flower-scented winds that blew from sandhills and high heaths, from marsh and mere, from willow carrs far out on the green levels and from dark fir woods on the little hills of the lovely Isle of Lothingland.

But Borrow, alas, was blind. He went striding out of his door on Oulton shore and was lost for weeks amid the mountains of Wales, the alien hills of Spain, leaving all beauty neglected at his feet.

But if that master of mighty prose turned his striding steps and vivid pen to other places, other scenes, leaving lesser men to stumble along paths that he neglected, we may count ourselves ten times more fortunate that the Norwich School of Painters preserved the beauty of his time, that their descendants to-day are painting the beauty which endures.

We may thank the landowners of ancient name, the merchant-princes of Norwich and the people, both high and humble, of East Norfolk, that this unique heritage has been preserved. Broadland owes a debt inexpressible to such men as the late Lord Lucas, the late Lord Desborough, Colonel Henry Cator of Woodbastwick Hall, Captain Tom Blofield of Hoveton House, Dr. Sydney Long, the late J. H. Gurney, and Major Anthony Buxton, to that robust Norfolker, Russell Colman, and to that quirkish, erudite, sardonic and lovable Norwicher, the late Walter Rye, who was a sort of James Horace Round in a minor key. To these and a score of others, alive and dead, England owes the preservation of ancient beauty in Norwich, the saving of present, living grace and life and wildness amid the rivers and meres of Broadland.

It will be a sad, bad day if ever this sanctuary of wild beauty and wild life is administered, not by local and loving hands, but by the dead, remote control of a Whitehall bureaucracy functioning with leprous touch through the cold alleys that lead to national ownership.

Broadland is too lovely, too vital and too individual a place ever to deserve the sad fate of becoming a nationalised "water-hikers' paradise". A little dredging here and there, the opening-up of grown-up broads, the control of sewage, a limit on the number of boats—these are desirable. They can be achieved by local co-operation, by the hands and brains of men who know and love their Norfolk scene.

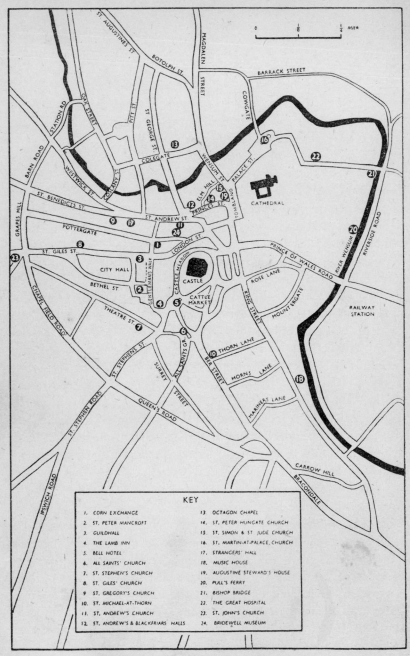

KEY

1. CORN EXCHANGE
2. ST. PETER MANCROFT
3. GUILDHALL
4. THE LAMB INN
5. BELL HOTEL
6. ALL SAINTS' CHURCH
7. ST. STEPHEN'S CHURCH
8. ST. GILES' CHURCH
9. ST. GREGORY'S CHURCH
10. ST. MICHAEL-AT-THORN
11. ST. ANDREW'S CHURCH
12. ST. ANDREW'S & BLACKFRIARS HALLS
13. OCTAGON CHAPEL
14. ST. PETER HUNGATE CHURCH
15. ST. SIMON & ST JUDE CHURCH
16. ST. MARTIN-AT-PALACE, CHURCH
17. STRANGERS' HALL
18. MUSIC HOUSE
19. AUGUSTINE STEWARD'S HOUSE
20. PULL'S FERRY
21. BISHOP BRIDGE
22. THE GREAT HOSPITAL
23. ST. JOHN'S CHURCH
24. BRIDEWELL MUSEUM

6 Street Plan of Norwich

Chapter
I

NORWICH
CITY OF GARDENS

---

*The Mystery of the Castle Mound
And the Glory of the Cathedral
A Place of Rivers*

7 Old houses near St. Helen's Church (*c.* 1383, rebuilt *c.* 1450), in the grounds of the Great Hospital, Bishopgate, Norwich

8 The Ship Inn in King Street, Norwich

9 Norwich Castle, classically refaced by Anthony Salvin in 1834

I

STAND on the battlemented roof of that huge square, keep(9)
which crowns the mighty and mysterious Castle Mound in the
heart of the city of Norwich and you gaze upon a city and a
landscape which are of the heart and soul of England. No city in
this kingdom is more truly English than Norwich. For it is a place
of great industries and yet, withal, great beauty. It is a country city,
set in an unspoiled countryside. Yet it produces great wealth from
trade and manufactures. It has a lovely soaring cathedral, yet is
bound by none of those decorous ecclesiastical spiders which spin
their stifling web about the streets of Durham and Ely, of Canterbury
and Salisbury. It has barracks and this squat and lowering castle
keep, but there is none of the air of a garrison town. It is a port to
which come sea-going ships, their iron hulls blistered with salt
spray—yet it is "The City of Gardens" through which rivers run,
sparkling like swords.

Stand, as I stood, upon the battlements of this ancient castle of the
Bigods, when the sun swims low in the west in a wild wrack of
wind-blown clouds. The sky is apple green, fading into umber and
yellow with a last blood-red flare to light the upper clouds, where
gulls are winnowing seaward. Gazing thus, from a lonely height
there lies below a tumbled sea of medieval roofs and stark factory
chimneys, the spires and towers of churches, the almost ethereal
beauty of the cathedral, the billow of green tree-tops. Through the
smoke and glitter of evening fires and early lights come the sudden
flashes of the rivers which gave birth to this city of the Eastern Angles
near two thousand years ago, before Christ walked in Galilee.
Looking upon it you will cease to wonder how it is that Norfolk is
perhaps the most individual of all English counties and Norwich
the mother of great English artists.

It would be easy to rhapsodise on the history and the beauties, on
the great men and imperishable artists which belong to Norwich if

one were Norfolk-born or Norwich-bred. Yet I will confess that, born in Suffolk, brought up in Cambridgeshire—and Cambridge, above all, is the true city of English loveliness—and dwelling long years in Essex with deep roots in all three counties, I can claim neither home nor ancestry in Norwich or Norfolk. But city and county alike took this chronicler in thrall more than forty years ago. That is the enchantment of Norfolk and its capital city. It is individual and, in a sense, unique.

For, within the compass of a man's vision from the top of this castle keep, there lie wild and shaggy heaths, heaths that inspired Borrow to immortal prose, that gave birth to the shining genius of Old Crome and the Norwich School of Painting—and, beyond the heaths, are massed woodlands, chequered fields of green and gold, the flashing shields of water which are the Broads, whose like is nowhere else in England, and, beyond it all, far to the east, the smoking chimneys and spidery masts of Yarmouth, the ancient town of herrings and ships, that "sits full upon the Maine Sea". In front of Yarmouth, glittering in the sun, is the long sweep of Breydon Water, the last echo of that great vanished estuary of Gariensis which, when Norwich was born, stretched well-nigh from the foot of the Castle Mound to the now-distant sweep and glitter of the North Sea.

Norwich took first shape as an ancient British settlement, a great sprawling village of that Icenic tribe called Cenomanni. They built it of wood and rammed earth, of wattle and reeds, at the western-most end of Gariensis where the dry land rose from vast and glittering marshes to a hinterland of forests and high heaths. The clear waters of Yare and Wensum, of Tud and Tas, there united in one. They gave fish and fresh water, grazing for cattle, rich flat lands for crops and gardens and, above all, protection from enemies. The swamps to the east were thunderous with the wings of wildfowl. The meres were whitened with the feathers of wild geese and duck. Spoonbills nested in the marsh carrs and raven and buzzard, peregrine and the great white-tailed eagle took toll of them.

As Kingsley wrote of the Fens in their undrained glory, so he might have written of Gariensis and the Broadland when Norwich was young:

The streams, too, abounded with pike, and the meres and stagnant waters swarmed with tench and carp.

Nor is there less plenty of water-fowl, and for a single halfpenny men can have enough for a full meal.

It was also facile to snare the crane, the heron, the wild-duck, teal, and the eccentric and most savoury snipe; the swallow-kite, the swarth raven, the hoary vulture, the swift eagle, the greedy goshawk and that grey beast, the wolf of the weald.

That, you will remember, was written in *The Camp of Refuge*, but in his enchanting and all-too-seldom-read *Prose Idylls* there comes this word picture, written of the Fens, but truer even of the Broadland:

... dark-green alders and pale-green reeds, stretched for miles round the broad lagoon, where the coot clanked and the bittern boomed and the sedge-bird, not content with its own sweet song, mocked the notes of all the birds around; while high overhead hung, motionless, hawk beyond hawk, buzzard beyond buzzard, kite beyond kite, as far as eye could see.

On the heaths and in the deep woods which spread over so much of the country to the north, the south and the west of early Norwich, there were wolves slinking like grey shadows; the tall red deer, rufous and challenging in their pride; fallow deer springing like dappled shadows across bracken-filled glades; the wild boar, grey-muzzled, rooting under the oaks and, in the bright streams, beavers built their dam.

When Aulus Plautius subdued those early Icenic builders of the stockaded wooden village, the sea ebbed and flowed through four great estuarine mouths which fed the salt and shallow waters of Gariensis. There was one opening at Horsey to the north-east, another at Kirkley near Lowestoft, a third at Lake Lothing and a four-mile-wide bay between Caister and Burgh Castle, of which Breydon is the last wild relic to-day.

The Romans christened Norwich "Venta Icenorum", and there they built a new and thriving settlement with a fort and garrison at Ad Tavum, which is now Tasburgh, to protect it with greater forts and larger garrisons at Caister and Burgh Castle.

The triremes and galleys with banked oars ploughed the waters and patrolled the estuary mouth to ward off the sea raiders and pirates who swept down in the kind months of summer from their Danish and Baltic roosts.

No man can say with certitude who built the first house and raised the first stockade on the lands that are now part of Norwich, but when Elizabeth the First paid a visit to the city, a local poet, searching his imagination, wrote this of the building of the first castle at Norwich:

> King Gurgunt I am hight, King Belin's eldest son,
> Whose sire, Dunwallo, first the British crown did wear.
> Whom truthless Gutlacke forced to pass the surging seas,
> His falsehood to revenge and Denmark laid to spoil,
> And finding in return this place a gallant vent,
> This castle fair I built . . .

King Gurgunt's connection with Norwich was slight enough in all conscience, but when we come to read the Anglo-Saxon Chronicle, there is a record in A.D. 1004 which says: "This year came Sweyne with his fleet to Norwich, plundering and burning the whole town" to such dreadful purpose that the townspeople of Norwich bought peace at the price of all available goods and gold. Then Sweyne's army, leaving their ships in Norwich waters, marched upon Thetford, which they set in flames. But by this time the forces of the East Anglian chieftains rallied, set upon them and drove them back, as they said themselves: "They never met with worse handplay in England than Ulf kytel brought them."

We may take it, I think, for granted that the great Castle Mound was there when Sweyne stormed and sacked the city. Its origin is unknown—a mighty mound of mystery reared by unknown hands at least a thousand years ago. Samuel Woodward says of the Castle Mound and the city about it:

No spot in the neighbourhood could have afforded the original founders of this fortress such advantages as this place presents; and these advantages can be fully appreciated only by examining the ground with the eye of a geologist. Reverting to the probable period when the Britons fixed on this spot as a place of security, two thousand years have elapsed. At that period the Yare and the Wensum were not the insignificant streams they now appear, but occupied the whole of the alluvial flat of their valleys, making that part of the present City Liberty in which the Castrum is placed a peninsula, leaving only a land-pass of about half a mile in width across the west, upon the ridge of which the present Dereham Road passes. And to add to its security the spot itself was in a corner, surrounded on nearly all sides by water; so that it is a matter of no surprise that a place thus fortified by nature should have been selected. This spot is one of the salient angles of the valley, having an elevation of about a hundred feet above the level of the river; the continuation of this level towards the south constitutes the Berg Street, now corruptly called Ber Street. The ballium on which the Castle stands is about twenty feet higher, raised, it is presumed, by art, with the soil of the inner ditch.

We may take it, therefore, that the Castle Mound is the original heart and fortified centre of the first Ancient British village from which the great city of Norwich, to-day a place of 115,000 inhabitants, has sprung.

Walter White, when he was writing *Eastern England* in the early 'sixties, said of the Norwich of our grandfathers, then a place of no more than 75,000 inhabitants, that it was said to occupy more ground than any other town of equal population in the kingdom, "which", he added:

you will perhaps believe when you see how large a part of its awkward thoroughfares consists of low mean houses, some still roofed with their ancient thatch. To build houses side by side, instead of one above the other, should be favourable to public health; but the dirt and squalor in some parts of this old city more than neutralise the structural advantage; and the multiplication of low houses imparts a poverty of aspect. It was for this reason, perhaps, that my first impression of the general mean appearance of Norwich was confirmed by all my subsequent visits.

A city however which contains a cathedral and six-and-thirty churches, besides other remarkable buildings, and still shows some portion of its mediaeval black flint wall, which for many generations has been famous for good singing and music, and a resolute will for religious freedom, cannot fail to be interesting.

But with what a feeling of bewilderment you plunge into its confusion of narrow, crooked, and hilly streets and lanes; now discovering half-a-dozen churches within a stone's throw of each other; now emerging into one or other of the irregular open spaces, thirteen in number, which the natives call Plains, St. Paul's Plain, Theatre Plain, Bank Plain, and so forth, where you pause for a moment after your many ins and outs, and ups and downs, and catch a few perspective effects along the narrow ways.

Now you are among weavers and shoe-makers; now in a crowd of "factory mawthers" to whom succeed dignitaries of the church, and gentle folk from hall and manor house for miles around, and groups of chubby-cheeked rustics talking in their queer dialect. With Winchester or Lichfield in your mind,

Norwich will appear in striking contrast. A cathedral town without drowsiness, and where noisy factories disturb the ecclesiastical quiet, but have not yet produced the distressing ugliness of the manufacturing towns of Yorkshire and Lancashire, is a remarkable phenomenon in these days.

One phrase of that Victorian description still is true of Norwich, "a cathedral town without drowsiness . . . where noisy factories . . . have not yet produced the distressing ugliness of the manufacturing towns of Yorkshire and Lancashire". This dual quality of beauty and business which was "a remarkable phenomenon" in White's day, is no less a phenomenon in our day.

The core and centre of the architectural beauty of Norwich is the cathedral(1). Ninety-two years after Sweyne laid waste the old Saxon city with fire and sword, there came to Norwich that highly individual, strong-willed churchman, Bishop Herbert de Losinga, who, having committed an act of simony, by no means uncommon in his day, made his peace with Pope and King and, in expiation, set about building that magnificent cathedral which is almost entirely his personal monument, for the greater part was finished in fifty years under his own supervision.

It is a great and noble church, 461 feet long and 72 feet broad, with a spire which soars 315 feet into the blue Norfolk skies.

Herbert de Losinga was a man of outstanding character, of far-seeing and statesmanlike powers, of great will and driving force.

Alas, nothing remains of his tomb, for the Puritans, those narrow-minded hypocrites, destroyed it during the Civil War. But there is an inscription on a slab which, since it tells the testimony of his time to his virtues, is worth quoting:

A MAN IMBUED WITH EVERY
SORT OF LEARNING
OF INCOMPARABLE ELOQUENCE
HANDSOME IN PERSON
AND OF BRIGHT COUNTENANCE
SO THAT THESE, WHO KNEW HIM NOT
MIGHT GUESS HE WAS A BISHOP
ONLY FROM LOOKING AT HIM

His "incomparable eloquence" was, I think, never bettered than

when he addressed a letter to the monks engaged upon building the
great piers and arches of his cathedral. It is such a letter as should be
written to-day to those regiments of idle bureaucrats who fatten on

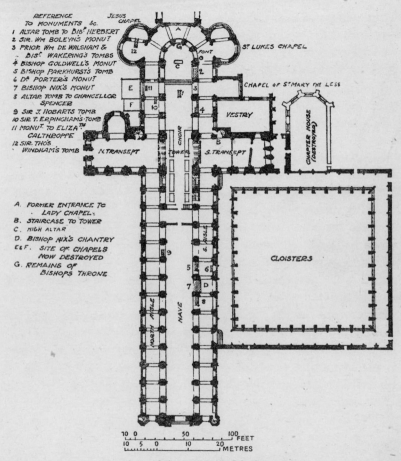

10 Plan of the Cathedral before 1869

this country's diminishing wealth, retard its slow recovery and beat
down its battered spirit. This is what Losinga wrote to those idle
and useless monks:

I love you and I am striving to deliver you, slow and indolent as you are, out
of the hands of the divine severity. Often have I stirred you up in person by

29

reminding you both privately and publicly of your duty in this respect, to apply yourselves fervently and diligently to the work of your church and to show carefulness in that work as done under the inspection of God's own eyes.

I was wont to entreat and to persuade you and would that I had succeeded in convincing your minds how great is the sincerity with which God must be served! But alas! The work drags on, and in providing materials you show no enthusiasm.

Behold the servants of the king and mine are really earnest in the works allotted to them. They gather stones, carry them to the spot and fill with them fields and ways, houses and courts.

You meanwhile are asleep with folded hands, numbed, as it were, and frost bitten by a winter of negligence, shuffling and failing in your duty through a paltry love of ease.

The clerestory was rebuilt in 1362, six years after the Black Prince led the chivalry of England to victory on the field of Poitiers. Bishop Thomas Percy, who had then been six years Bishop of Norwich, was its builder.

The cathedral had already been the scene of a bloody riot in which part of the splendid and spacious cloister was destroyed in a fight between the citizens of Norwich and the monks in 1272. The cloister was completed, much later, in 1450, and it thus displays several different styles of stonework and tracery from fourteenth-century work in the Eastern Walk up to mid-fifteenth-century work(13). The north wall of the cloister shows a remarkable display of arms of the descendants of blood, or in office, of the great families who attended Queen Elizabeth when she dined in the cloisters in 1578. Among the arms are those of Hastings, de Grey, Bacon and others, whose names are still potent in the everyday life of Norfolk to-day.

There is much that is unique in Norwich Cathedral. Its outstanding distinction is that it possesses the least changed Norman ground plan of any great English church. Moreover, much of the original Norman work remains. The lantern of the central tower is Norman, the great nave and transept remain as they were built, whilst the presbytery and choir retain the Norman plan, with three projecting chapels to the east.

Seen from the outside, the cathedral rises above the low roofs of these chapels, the choir dominating them, with the magnificent

11 Norwich Cathedral: the Norman Nave. The lierne vaulting of the roof
was built after the fire of 1463

12 St. Luke's Chapel with its Norman arcading and fourteenth century font

13 The Cloister, with its splendid fifteenth-century vault and early fourteenth-century window tracery

NORWICH CATHEDRAL

tower and spire thrusting skywards in a vision of power and grace. The four sides of the tower contain about a hundred delicate arches and windows with much graceful tracery in stone, most of it in diamond and ring pattern. The work is Norman, but the spire is fifteenth century. The west front is also Norman and the original Norman arch remains in the central doorway, whilst the aisle fronts are also Norman.

When one enters the cathedral, the majestic grace and soaring beauty of the interior are breathtaking. The walls rise in triple tiers of Norman arcading(11), broken by two immense round pillars and two four-centred arches on the south side. The triforium is unique in that it is almost as lofty as the main arcade.

The roof of the nave, seventy feet above one, is carved with hundreds of men, women, animals and angels, and in the fourteen bays of the nave are hundreds of bosses, of which altogether there are more than 1,200 in the cathedral. These, with the unique collections of sculptured figures in the cloister, are unrivalled elsewhere in England.

The carvings in the fourteen bays depict a multitude of Bible incidents and stories from the Creation of Life to the story of the Ark, the Tower of Babel, Rebecca at the Well, the tale of Jacob and Esau, Joseph in Egypt, the Birth of Moses, Samson and Delilah, Solomon in all his glory, the Birth of Jesus, and so to the Crucifixion, the Resurrection, the Ascension and, in the last bay of all, the Day of Judgment. Bishop Lyhart built this outstanding roof five centuries ago. His stone screen contains much delicate and lovely work and his grave beneath the screen is marked by a blue stone.

Bishop Losinga built the little Norman chapel of St. Luke(12), which is oddly round in shape, like its companion, the Jesus Chapel. St. Luke's is now the parish church of St. Mary's-in-the-Marsh, the old church of which was destroyed some four centuries ago. The Jesus Chapel has been greatly restored, but it contains an old altar stone and a unique brass to Randolph Pulverton, who was Master of the Charnel House in the fifteenth century. Relics are said to have been kept under the old altar stone and also on top of a very odd-looking low arch built across the aisle, which one reaches by a spiral stairway.

The greatest treasure in the cathedral is a painting on wood, which can be seen in the south aisle of the ambulatory. Once it was a reredos in the Jesus Chapel and, like so much other "idolatrous" work of beauty, it would obviously have been destroyed by the Puritans had they discovered it. It was either removed or stolen, just in time, by someone who turned it upside down, put four legs on it and used it as a table. As such it remained until the late Professor Willis discovered it about a hundred years ago.

The painting is said to have been the work of Thomas de Okell, a prominent citizen, who possibly painted the exquisite little Wilton Diptych now in the National Gallery. It is divided into five panels which depict the Scourging of our Lord, the Bearing of the Cross, the Crucifixion, the Resurrection and the Ascension. The design and colouring are bold in execution and brilliant in tone. The fact that the picture bears the arms of "the Fighting Bishop", Henry Spencer, is significant, for a relative of the Bishop owned the Wilton Diptych. Altogether this painting is an out-standing work, particularly in its lifelike depiction of the expressions on the faces of our Lord, the Madonna, the soldiers and the sadistic ruffian charged with the duty of scourging Christ.

The ambulatory contains treasures of unique interest, including a grant on parchment by Losinga, another by Hugh Bigod, a fourteenth-century Domesday Book of the diocese, the great Bible in red morocco on which Queen Victoria signed her Coronation oath, a gold ring of the thirteenth century and the oaken-carved head of Bishop Lyhart's pastoral staff. Then there are two little wooden men in trousers, who are shown in the act of striking a bell with swords. These Jacobean relics once formed part of an old clock and are placed under a modern clock in the south transept.

The cathedral also possesses what is believed to be the finest collection extant of 1,500 rolls of the Obedientiars, who were the twelve departmental executives responsible to the Prior, together with some 2,000 manor rolls and accounts, many belonging to the thirteenth and fourteenth centuries. The rolls of the Obedientiars are from one to ten feet in length, and it is said that if they were placed end to end they would stretch for a mile and a half.

Famous men who sleep in the cathedral include old Sir Thomas

Erpingham, that doughty warrior whom Shakespeare immortalised; Bishop Bathurst, who, in his time, was the only Liberal bishop in the House of Lords and is commemorated in a good monument by Chantrey; Sir John Hobart, the Tudor Attorney-General; Sir Thomas Wyndham, a Counsellor of Henry VII and many bishops. They include William de Turbe, the only bishop who dared champion Becket against Henry; "the Fighting Bishop", Spencer, who lived in Chaucer's time; "jocular Corbet", son of a Surrey gardener, poet and wit and Chaplain to James I, whose drinking bouts in the wine cellar with his Chaplain are still on record; Bishop Wakering, persecutor of the Lollards, whose tomb bears ten figures on pedestals, and Bishop Goldwell, who is commemorated, not only by his magnificent tomb, but in the "gold wells" which decorate the lavish display of starlike bosses in the lovely vault of the presbytery.

To my mind the outstanding single work in stone in the cathedral is the magnificent tomb of Bishop Goldwell. He built the spire, his lasting memorial, and is commemorated in this singularly lovely tomb, a well-nigh perfect example of fifteenth-century craftsmanship in stone and painted decoration. The tomb is pure Gothic beauty, unequalled in this country. Not many years ago it was redecorated in all its original brilliance of glowing colours, through the generosity of members of the British Association. The Bishop lies, life-size in stone, wearing his processional cope over his vestments—the only monument of its kind in England that survived the Reformation. His feet are on a crouching lion, jewelled gloves upon his hands, and his features, although defaced, still give dignity to the magnificence of his robed figure.

The Bishop's Throne, which is unique in Western Europe, stands under the middle arch of the apse and thus reproduces the arrangement of the Basilica or Roman Imperial law courts, where the Judge (or Praetor) sat in the centre of the apse on a raised tribunal with his officers about him. The backcloth on the throne, embroidered in gold thread, was worked by Queen Mary. The apse is the finest Norman example in the whole of England, which is not so unique a distinction as it sounds, for there is only one other at Peterborough which, to my mind, cannot come near Norwich. The sixty-two monastic stalls, with their small carved misericords and the canopies above them, are exquisite fifteenth-century work.

The carvings include sleeping dogs, pelicans, eagles, human faces and an attractive company of girls with, as arm-rests, birds, a crowned king, grotesque faces and miniature gargoyles. The carving of these stalls is among the best in the cathedral. It is superb crafts-manship, overlooked by far too many visitors. The misereres, for example, include a squirrel eating nuts, a man riding on a pig, a monkey on a dog's back, a knight in armour, monks, dragons, a mermaid and a man opening the jaws of a lion. In another carving an old woman with a spindle and distaff is flying screaming after a fox which is departing at the gallop with her chicken, whilst, behind her back, her pig has taken the opportunity to rob her three-legged cooking-pot. Another shows a monk giving bread to schoolboys with their books wide open on the table. Then there is a captivating view of a shepherd tending his flock—altogether an enchanting gallery of whimsical scenes, expressive faces and imaginative oddities, carved by men who were alive when Agincourt was fought.

The cloister, as I have said, was badly damaged in the riot of 1272, but in its completed form to-day, it is the biggest monastic cloister in England and the only one with a top story.

As one enters from the singularly lovely Prior's Door one sees the sudden vision of this impressive quadrangle, whose walks are 12 feet wide, with a garth 145 feet square. Arthur Mee has rightly described these walks as "like avenues of stone trees touched with bronze, russet and gold, with clustered shafts for trunks, vaulting for overhanging boughs and glorious coloured bosses, hanging as if they might be fruit or flowers".

In the upper story of the cloister are a number of small rooms, one of which has been turned into the cathedral library. Among the 7,000 rare books and manuscripts is the Berners Book, printed by Wynkyn de Worde, Caxton's foreman on Caxton's own press. In the cloister itself are two small but exceedingly good statues of George V and Queen Mary, the work of Gilbert Ledward.

From whatever outdoor angle one looks at this incredibly lovely cathedral, it enchants the eye by the impressive beauty of its design, the soaring majesty and grace of tower and spire and the astonishing diversity of exterior carving, sculpture and the delicacy of many of the windows.

In a quiet, green corner at the east end of the building, called Life's Green, lies the simple grave of Edith Cavell, that martyr of the First World War, who was shot by the German Army one autumn night in 1915 because she had dared to help British Troops.

The inscription on her grave, her last words before the fatal volley rang out, enshrines the very spirit of Christianity:

Standing as I do, in view of God and Eternity, I realise that patriotism is not enough; I must have no hatred or bitterness toward anyone.

A second after she had spoken those words the rattle of musketry shattered the autumn dusk and she fell, riddled with bullets. Her tomb of green grass, with the simple cross above it, is the most significant of all amid the grandeur of the ages which surrounds it and soars in stone into her beloved Norfolk sky.

D. Hodgson, del.   S. Williams, sc.

Bishop's Bridge, Norwich.

14 *Reproduced from an Engraving of 1830*

Chapter
II

THE
NORWICH PAINTERS

From "Old Crome" to Munnings
Churches of Beauty and a Monstrous City Hall
Kett and Borrow

II

WHEN the Conqueror planted his iron foot on the neck
of Saxon England and reared stone castles to subdue her
people, the great mound that had been the mysterious
heart of early Norwich for perhaps a thousand years was the obvious
place on which to plant a fortress. There, soon after Senlac had been
fought, William FitzOsbert built the first castle. Nothing is left
to-day but its foundations.

The present keep and entrance tower, standing squarely like a
great embattled cube(9), was built early in the twelfth century by
the powerful Bigods. Its white stone Norman walls, glittering
newly in the bright sun, earned it the name of Blanchflower. It has
no great military history. True, the Flemings stormed and took it in
1174 and French troops held it in the days of King John, but from
the thirteenth century to the nineteenth the castle of Blanchflower,
outwardly white and glistening, inwardly was a dark prison, a grim
house of bondage for wretched men chained to the walls in dungeons
deep in the black foundations.

Then, just over a century ago, it was refaced by Anthony Salvin
and, having been acquired by the city, the late King George V,
when Duke of York, opened it in 1894 as the Norwich Castle
Museum.

And thus, indeed, it fulfils a splendid purpose, for nowhere in
England is there a better museum in the cities of her shires and
counties. It tells the story of Norwich and of Norfolk throughout
the centuries. There are relics of Nelson, who was son of a Norfolk
parson and educated at the little fourteenth-century grammar school
hard by the cathedral. There is the Tudor Room, with its glowing
tapestries made in the city by Flemish weavers when Henry VII was
on the throne, and the Elizabethan Room which has fine panelling
and a glorious moulded ceiling, and the Georgian Room which is
just what you would expect a Georgian room to be, and a long

shovelboard table and a glove which belonged to one of the Pastons, old pottery, silver and plate, and, to crown the oddities of civic history, Old Snap, the dragon in scarlet and gold who, for 400 years, traversed the city in procession and snapped his jaws at the gaping crowds. There is a dress of cream silk, high-waisted and striped with pale green, which belonged to Marie Antoinette, and a tiny bodice which fitted the small waist of that sad queen.

There is, too, a great diorama, which shows you Norwich as it was in 1720, with its sea of gabled houses, the grim castle and soaring cathedral, its alley-ways and Bishop's Bridge, and the old watergate at Pull's Ferry, where the Priors landed from their barges. Dotted here and there, amid the jumble of roofs and warrens of narrow streets, are the towers and spires of the six-and-thirty churches whose chiming bells made windy music in the clouds.

The true glory of this museum lies not in these relics of great citizens, interiors from fine houses or survivals of ancient arts and crafts, but in the splendid art gallery and the natural history museum, quite, I think, the finest of its kind outside London.

The Norwich School of Painting was founded by John Crome, the weaver's son, whose landscapes, some painted with hairs taken from his cat's tail because he was too poor to buy brushes, are worth thousands. Crome began life in a dirty little beer-house in a poky back street of old Norwich. Paint was in his blood but money was not in his pocket. He began to earn his miserable living as a sign-painter's apprentice. On long summer evenings, when his work was done, he would walk out to Mousehold Heath and paint oak trees and sunsets, sandy lanes, may blossom in bloom and a windmill against the sky, using an oyster-shell for a palette.

I think of William Beechey's description, when he was about twenty years old: "a very awkward, uninformed, country lad but extremely shrewd in all his remarks upon art, though he wanted words and terms to express his meaning".

And then you remember George Borrow's forthright words to a brother artist upon whom he rammed home the truth that there was no need to look abroad for models. Borrow exclaimed, as my friend Sir Alfred Munnings, that greatest Norfolk artist of to-day, might well have exclaimed in his downright English:

A living master? Why there he comes! thou hast had him long, he has long guided thy young hand towards the excellence which is yet far from thee, but which thou canst attain if thou shouldst persist and wrestle, even as he has done, midst gloom and despondency—ay, and even contempt; he who now comes up the creaking stair to thy little studio in the second floor to inspect thy last effort before thou departest, the little stout man whose face is very dark, and whose eye is vivacious; that man has attained excellence, destined some day to be acknowledged, though not till he is cold and his mortal part returned to its kindred clay. He has painted, not pictures of the world but English pictures, such as Gainsborough himself might have done; beautiful rural pictures, with trees which might well tempt the little birds to perch upon them; thou needst not run to Rome, brother, where lives the old Mariolater, after pictures of the world, whilst at home there are pictures of England; nor needst thou even go to London, the big city, in search of a master, for thou hast one at home in the old East Anglian town who can instruct thee whilst thou needst instruction; better stay at home, brother, at least for a season, and toil and strive, 'midst groanings and despondency, till thou has attained excellence even as he has done—the little dark man with the brown coat and the topboots; whose name will one day be considered the chief ornament of the old town, and whose works will at no distant period rank amongst the proudest pictures of England—and England against the world!—thy master, my brother, thy, at present all too little considered master—CROME.

How true Borrow was has been proved by the appreciation of succeeding generations. To John Crome we owe the genesis and inspiration of the Norwich School, the one important School of Painting in England, which takes its name and character from a city and its surroundings. Crome was born in Norwich in 1768 and died in the city in 1821. Almost his whole life and works were influenced by Norwich and its immediate countryside. He was not drawn to London or the Continent nor did he seek fashionable patronage of the sort which put Gainsborough, Romney and others on the road to fame. Crome was as individual as his own Norfolk, and as sturdily independent.

So strong was his influence on the art and daily life of Norwich that on February 19th, 1803, a group of his pupils, patrons and friends met and formed the "Norwich Society for the purpose of an Enquiry into the Rise, Progress and present state of Painting, Architecture & Sculpture, with a view to point out the Best Methods of study to attain to Greater Perfection in these Arts". Two years later the first exhibition pictures by the School was held in Sir

Benjamin Wrench's Court which stood where the present Corn Exchange now is. Eighteen artists exhibited 223 paintings in oils and water-colours. So successful was the exhibition that it became an annual affair. Thus Norwich achieved the distinction of being the first city outside London to hold an annual exhibition of Works of Art. Crome's principal patrons were the Gurneys of Earlham Hall, that enchantingly peaceful house set in its riverside park just outside the city. He went with them to Wales once only, and once to Paris. The result of the first visit was that superb picture "Slate Quarries", now in the Tate Gallery. The Paris visit produced two remarkable pictures of unusual style and distinction, "The Boulevard des Italiennes" and the "Fishmarket, Boulogne". Both were purchased by Mr. J. J. Gurney and are still owned by the family.

These three pictures give one a profound insight into the potentialities of Crome. Quite clearly he was influenced in his early life by certain Dutch painters, notably the Ruisdaels, Hobbema, Koninck, and the incomparable Cuyp, but, after all, the scenery and surroundings which influenced those Dutch masters were very similar to the scenery and surroundings amid which Crome lived and worked. How often has one seen the soft, sunlit brilliance or evening nuances of colour, of which Cuyp was the master, over the river valleys and heathland of the Norwich scene? And the Broadland landscapes are the landscapes of Hobbema.

We may well ask ourselves, however, what would have been the outcome in new developments of style had Crome gone to Italy or spent a longer time in Paris. England then might have lost that unique distinction of style and colouring which is now the unmistakable hallmark of the Norwich School, whether its pictures were painted by Crome, John Sell Cotman(15), Henry Bright, David Hodgson, the Ladbrookes, Thomas Lound, Obadiah Short, the Stannards, James Stark or that lesser-known member of the School, W. Freeman, one of whose smaller pictures is among my most treasured possessions—an exquisite little gem of a Norfolk "loke", gay with blossom in spring, with two rustic figures ambling beside the broken palings of an old park fence into a valley distance, blue with that ineffable blue which is peculiar to the Norfolk scene.

Crome, or "Old Crome" as he is generally known, did not paint

15   Norwich: the Market Place in 1807
From a watercolour by J. S. Cotman

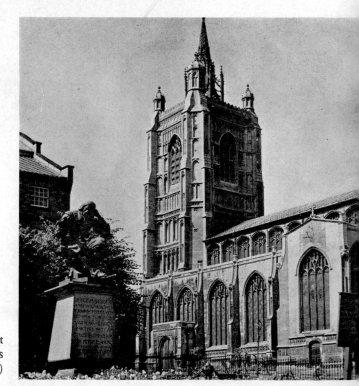

17 The monument
to Sir Thomas
Browne (1605-1682)

St. Peter Mancroft, Norwich (1430-1455)

46

more than about 300 pictures, but he was a pioneer in reviving original etching in England. Much of his time was taken up in teaching. His portrait, by John Opie, shows him with that "spark of divine fire" which influenced so many of his pupils and thereby put England in his debt for ever.

His son, John Berney Crome, George Vincent and James Stark ("Stark of Norwich") followed most closely in his footsteps. Much of their work is almost indistinguishable to the casual eye from that of "Old Crome" himself. For that we can be grateful. The four of them caught and preserved for all time the ancient and medieval charm of old Norwich, the forest-like beauty of its surrounding woods with their stag-headed oaks and sandy "lokes", whilst Stannard, the Cotmans, and later in our own time, Sir Arnesby Brown have preserved the Dutch-like beauty of the Norfolk waterways with their windmills and heavy-sailed wherries, their marching willows and glorious sweep of sky. "Moonrise on the Yare", by "Old Crome", is not merely a picture in a thousand. It is unique.

This is no place for a lengthy disquisition upon the beauties and unique individualism of the Norwich School. The visitor to Norwich may see them in the Norwich Castle Museum and he should most certainly not miss the new Colman Art Gallery.

But I think if "Old Crome" were to gaze upon his native city he would today see it much as in his own time, "The City of Churches" and "The City in an Orchard". The gorse-clad rise of Mousehold Heath is, luckily, a public place, not so very different from the day when the Old Master painted his picture of this name. There are still windmills in the bright valley of the Yare and old oaks standing by pools which match Crome's "Poringland Oak", which you may see in the National Gallery, with that other of his masterpieces, "The Windmill on Mousehold Heath", which has all the lonely beauty and sun-filled space of the Norfolk scene.

There lies still at the foot of the Castle Mound the open space of the cattle market, largest in any English city—a visible reminder that Norwich and England alike depend, in the long run, upon farms and farmers for their strength. Beyond and below lies the open

Market Place(15), dominated by the magnificent fifteenth-century church of St. Peter Mancroft(17) and the equally lovely but smaller fifteenth-century Guildhall. Norwich Market Place, with its gaily striped stalls, where you may buy anything from flowers to fish, from rabbits to bootlaces, from old books to ancient silver, has a continental air. It is such a scene of busy, coloured activity as one might have seen in the Middle Ages. It belongs almost to a French city or, as I prefer it, to a Dutch market.

But, alas and alack, this great Market Place with its exquisite Guildhall, its magnificent church and its gracious Queen Anne buildings, is dominated, overshadowed, cast down and almost bullied out of countenance by a mighty new Gibraltar of brick, the City Hall. What shall we say of it? What, indeed, would "Old Crome" have said. This factory-like block with its factory-like chimney of a tower possesses, as I have written elsewhere,[1] "the proportions of a brick and the complexion of Brown Windsor soap".

An official guide to Norwich says of this monolithic monstrosity, "this municipal enterprise, calling for a vast faith in the future of the city, involved the destruction of many period buildings over a large area". Further comment is unnecessary.

Norwich Market Place was begun by the Normans. It superseded the earlier Saxon trading centre, known as Tombland, still a place of architectural delight, with its pebbled surface, its shady trees and its magnificent gateways, the Erpingham Gate and the St. Ethelbert Gate, which pierce the fortress-like walls of the cathedral precincts. Luckily the vandals have not been busy with their "vast faith in the future" in Tombland, which has nothing to do with tombs but derives its name from the ancient "Thum" or open land, the fair-stead at the monastery gates. Who would not be enchanted by the medieval names which distinguished the various parts of the Market Place, The Spicery, Herb Market, Pudding Lane, The Butchery, Soper Lane and Worstead Row, which took its name from that Norfolk village of Worstead where worsted was carded and spun.

The Georgian history of the Market Place is prettily preserved in

[1] *Marshland Adventure*, Geo. Harrap & Co. Ltd., 1950.

The Gentlemen's Walk, an immediate picture of Georgian bucks in long-skirted coats with silver buttons, silken hose and silver-buckled shoes, sunning themselves on leisurely mornings when carriages pass and the internal-combustion engine, "the suicide of man", was unborn. It is "a short trot", as they say in Norfolk, from the Market Place to the Haymarket with its medieval merchant's house known as Curat's House and the statue of Sir Thomas Browne(17), the author of *Religio Medici*, that careful naturalist, philosopher and seeker-out of medieval lore, whose house stood in front of the present Lamb Inn Yard on a site now marked by a tablet at No. 12 Orford Place.

The near-by Orford Hill was once the old Hog Market. There stands the ancient Bell Hotel and near by is the equally ancient Westlegate, with a vista of All Saints Church, which is picturesque, but not to be compared with the church of St. Stephen by Rampant Horse Street. The porch of St. Stephen dates from about 1350, the tower from 1610, and the church contains some really good stained glass and brasses.

St. Peter Mancroft(16) is, however, the church of churches. It is said to have taken its name from the "Magna Crofta", or big croft or meadow, which is now the Market Place. It was begun in 1430, finished in 1455, is 212 feet long and 90 feet wide with a nave 60 feet high, whilst the west tower is nearly 100 feet high, topped by a nineteenth-century spire, which rises to a height of 146 feet. The glass in the east window is a glorious display of fifteenth-century work, brilliant as jewels. This is one of the priceless treasures of Norwich. St. Peter Mancroft is full of rich and beautiful work in wood and stone, not least of which is the splendid and unusual roof of the nave and chancel, much of it fan-traceried in timber with a richly carved cornice containing some forty angels bearing shields and emblems. The peal of twelve bells and a tenor is the best in the city and on Tuesday nights it fills the sky with unforgettable music.

St. Gregory's is another good fourteenth-century church standing near the Market Place, containing among other things a brass eagle lectern with three lions at the base, dated 1493, one of the oldest lecterns in England. The finest display of church brasses in Norwich, however, is in St. John Maddermarket, a fifteenth-century building with some fourteenth-century remnants. The brasses commemorate the family of John Terry, who was mayor in 1523, and other mayors and citizens; an almost unique collection which luckily survived the vandalism of past centuries.

Just above the Market Place stands the church of St. Giles, founded in the time of William the Conqueror, rebuilt at the end of the fourteenth century and dominated by a tower 113 feet high, which was a beacon in the sixteenth century. There are several good brasses in this church.

It is impossible to detail all the thirty or more churches of the city, but the bombed St. Michael-at-Thorn, mainly fifteenth century, was interesting inasmuch that it stood amid sixteen thorn trees, clearly descendants of the thicket of thorns in which the original church was reared.

A great church, second only to St. Peter Mancroft, is St. Andrew's(20), full of good old glass, much good carving, and containing the great canopied tomb of Sir John and Lady Suckling, parents of the poet. It is a splendid tomb of the Elizabethan period. The Sucklings were forebears of Nelson, who was a pupil of Norwich Grammar School and worshipped in this church. Their old home, Suckling House, with a splendid trussed roof, stands near the east end of the church, and dates from earlier than the time of the Black Death. The old house is now a public hall. Facing it is an interesting building, known as Armada House, which is dated 1589, but may easily be somewhat older.

Opposite St. Andrew's Church is St. Andrew's Hall(19), part of the original great Dominican church, which was rebuilt by Sir Thomas Erpingham. St. Andrew's Hall is 126 feet long and nearly 70 feet wide, with a magnificent hammer-beam roof, a splendid range of twenty-eight clerestory windows and a portrait gallery which includes the last portrait of Nelson before his death, painted by Sir William Beechey. There is a splendid Gainsborough of Sir Harbord Harbord, Lord Suffield of Gunton, two pictures by Opie of mayors and a Victorian portrait of Sir J. J. Colman, the mustard king, by that almost forgotten Victorian artist, Sir Hubert von Herkomer. Near by is Blackfriars Hall, another part of the original Dominican church, but larger than many present-day churches. Therein Sir Thomas Browne was knighted by Charles II. It also has a portrait gallery.

A small and most lovely little chapel which, I confess, I only discovered when writing this inadequate book, is the Octagon Chapel at the back of Colegate, a work of the elegant Thomas Ivory, who built it in 1756—a building, as a contemporary writer said, "justly admired for the heathen irregularity of its structure as well as for its internal decorations"(23).

If I wish to go to church in Norwich without saying my prayers, I turn my steps towards St. Peter Hungate, which stands at the top of Elm Hill, a gem of an old church which is now a museum of church art. In it you will find a good collection of church plate; much medieval carving from screens, pews and arches; a most delicate silver cross decorated with a ball of Blue John and amethysts; Wycliffe's Bible of 1380; certain fiddles, flutes and a hand organ of the sort that were used in village churches in our grand-father's day, and three supremely lovely "Books of Hours". One is Flemish and another French, both of them fifteenth century, and a third is East Anglian and a hundred years older. Their colouring is brilliant.

Now Elm Hill(4), which is no hill at all but a narrow cobbled street with a little open place at the top end, where stands the "Britons Arms," thatched and Elizabethan, once the oldest inn in Norwich, but now, alas, without a licence, is a perfect medieval street. I doubt if it can be equalled or surpassed in any town or city in England. Practically all its buildings are of the fifteenth and sixteenth centuries. Nearly all are well preserved. Therein you may buy good pictures, with often a find from the Norwich School, at the Elm Hill Gallery of my friend, Mr. Roy Nightingale, or you may purchase old furniture, Persian rugs, pewter and old silver, or buy a dog or, if you are lucky and favoured, be entertained by one of the more reputable citizens of Norwich in the Stranger's Club. There, indeed, is a splendid old building occupying much of one side of the street, full of good old timber, carving and furniture, with vast, open fireplaces on which one could roast a calf or burn half a tree.

Elm Hill was a fashionable place in the fifteenth century and the

Pastons had a house there. John Pettus, who was mayor in 1590, also had a house, which lately has been restored to something of its ancient glory. Indeed, although we may condemn the Norwich Corporation for destroying so much old property by the Market Place and erecting thereon that City Hall which looks like a cross between a power station and a Teutonic barracks, we may give praise to them for having purchased and reconditioned most of the property in Elm Hill at a time when an agitation was on foot to pull down the lot. True, the City Fathers were prodded into doing so by the Norwich Society. A pity the society could not have influenced better the choice of the City Hall.

At the foot of Elm Hill where it joins Wensum Street stands the sad and ruinous little church of St. Simon and St. Jude, mainly fourteenth- and fifteenth-century work. Its principal interest is that, in the chancel, there lie in one grave the bodies of four knights who were killed in the great fight on Mousehold Heath when Robert Kett, the tanner of Wymondham, marched on Norwich with his rebel army in protest against the appalling rise in the cost of living. Kett was hanged from the castle walls. Many of his men are buried in the church of St. Martin-at-Palace, near which Lord Sheffield was killed. St. Martin's is the only church in Norwich round which you can drive.

Kett's Rebellion is one of the most shameful episodes in English history. It stamps the final infamy upon the sadistic reign of that cruel and covetous Tudor, Henry VIII. One has only to gaze upon Holbein's portrait of that bloated monarch and see the small pig-eyes, the thin, cruel lips and the vulturine nose of a man, diseased in body, besotted with egoism, to realise that under such a tyrant there could be no freedom of mind or body in an England under his heel.

Every school-child knows of his spoliation of the monasteries, the slaughter of his wives and the hoggishness of his table manners, but how many remember the story of that sad day in the summer of 1549, when the Norfolk rustics, sick of the abuse of the liberties of Church and State, marched under Kett through Norwich to Mousehold Heath. Kett, a man of some education and upright principles, converted the Earl of Surrey's great mansion in Norwich into a jail. Therein he clapped most of the leading gentlemen of the county, including the mayor of the city. Kett held a daily court of justice under a tree called the Oak of Reformation which has long since disappeared. From time to time the mayor was brought out of jail and obliged to assist at the court.

Twenty thousand men encamped under Kett on the Heath in turf huts roofed with boughs. Naturally, they were joined by all sorts of lawless characters glad to use the uprising as an excuse for pillage and robbery, but, as Froude rightly remarks: "Considering the wild character of the assemblage the order preserved was remarkable." Kett did his best to behave in a reasonable manner, but some of his followers indulged in excesses in the city.

Kett's petition to the King is a pathetic document. It deserves better recognition in English history. It was a recital of the grievances which the Norfolk peasants suffered as the result of the abolition of the monasteries, most of which had been centres of good employ-ment, charity, good doctoring and general benevolence. Their dissolution was followed by a land-grabbing campaign in which all-too-many great men seized common lands which were the rightful property of the village poor.

The petition pleaded that such enclosures should be prevented and that "rede-grounde and meadowe grounde may be at suche price as they were in the first yere of King henry the seventh; that all bushells within your realm be of one stice, that is to say, to be in measure eight gallons; that prests or vicars that be not able to preche and sett forth the woorde of God to hys parisheners may be thereby putt from hys benyfice; that all bonde men may be ffre, for God made all ffre with hys precious blode sheddyng; that all ryvers may be ffre and common to all men for fyshyng and passage; that the pore mariners or fyshermene may have whole profights of their fyshyngs as purpses [porpoises], grampes [grampuses], whalles, or any grett fyshe, so it be not prejudicall to your grace"; that in every parish someone might be appointed to "teche pore mens chyldren of ther paryshe the boke called the Cathakysme and the prymer".

Every reform asked was fair and reasonable. It is incredible that neither King, Privy Council nor Parliament could devise means whereby to meet these requests with reasonable compromise rather than by bloodshed. Henry, however, regarded the petition as a personal affront. He promised that if the men went home and got in the harvest he would ask Parliament to see what reforms could be granted. Kett, we believe, was willing to do so. Many of his followers, however, had got out of hand and were pillaging the country. Then, on a July day, a herald arrived promising pardon to all who would return to their homes. Kett replied: "Kings are wont to pardon wicked persons—not innocent and just men. We have done nothing to deserve such pardon and have been guilty of no crime. We, therefore, despise such idle speeches as unprofitable to our purpose."

Thereupon the Privy Council sent troops, under the Marquis of Northampton. They were defeated by the rebels, who fought so fiercely that they were described as "half dead, drowned in their own and other men's bloud, even to the last gasp, furiously withstood our men when they could scarce hold their weapons. Yea, many also strooken thorow the brests with swordes and the synewes of their legs cut asunder, yet creeping on their knees, were mooved with such furie, as they wounded our souldiers lying amongst the slaine, almost without life".

That is the Norfolk spirit.

After this defeat the Privy Council ordered the Earl of Warwick, who was on his way to Scotland with an expeditionary force mainly of foreign mercenaries, to march on Norwich. He breached the city walls and, after a lot of hand-to-hand street fighting in which bands of armed peasants slew many of his men and the narrow alley-ways ran red with blood, Kett's men were driven on to Mousehold Heath. There, at Dussyns Dale, they made a last stand.

The battle was fought on an August day. The rebels set fire to their huts and, under the smoke cloud, furiously attacked the earl's army. He had received fresh reinforcements and was armed with artillery. Kett's men had none. The battle was fierce and bloody, but the trained foreign soldiers, fighting in ordered array, well armed and well armoured, cut them down.

We may picture that fearful battle, pathetic in its heroism and bloodshed—the great pall of smoke drifting over the heath from burning huts and blazing gorse bushes. Acres of fern and heather on fire and, through all the smoke and clang of battle, the screams of

18   The Strangers' Hall, Norwich (c. 1450)

19 St. Andrew's Hall, Norwich. Originally the nave of a Dominican Church (c. 1460)

20 St. Andrew's Church, Norwich (1606): Gothic font, Tudor font-cover, and eighteenth-century mural monuments

wounded, the battle-cries of German and Flemish soldiers, the clash of swords on armour, the intermittent thudding boom and flash of muzzle-loading cannon, culverins and hand-guns. Between 2,000 and 3,000 of Kett's men were slain. Kett himself escaped, but was caught next day in a barn at Swannington. He was taken to the Tower, brought back to Norwich and hanged from the walls of Blanchflower, the great white Norman keep, which still dominates the city of trees and churches. Nine of his principal lieutenants were hanged from the Oak of Reformation. Forty-five more were hung, drawn and quartered in Norwich Market Place. In all, 300 Norfolk men were executed for no greater crime than that they asked for justice and were prepared to fight for it. Such was the price paid by men who had pleaded that "pore men's chyldren" should be taught "the boke called the Cathakysme and the prymer". Such were the Norwich Martyrs, whose names find no place on the Roll of Martyrs. A plaque on the Castle Keep commemorates Kett.

Those are the sad and bloody memories of Norwich Market Place and of Mousehold Heath. For myself, I prefer to think of Borrow, that man of mighty heart and puissant pen, that greatest of all vagabonds of English literature, striding over Mousehold to meet "the wind on the heath, brother" or standing on Norwich Market Place amid just such a motley crowd of sun-tanned broadsmen, blue-jerseyed Yarmouth deep-sea fishermen, prosperous farmers, cunning higglers, ruddy-faced Norfolk squires, sly horse-dealers, furtive dog-stealers, chattering flower-sellers and straw-chewing drovers as you may see to-day, standing there seeking among the crowd for those true Norfolk gipsies whom he, Borrow, immortalised in prose and Alfred Munnings has immortalised in paint.

You may still see them in the back alleys of Norwich or forcing their way through the market crowd. These grandchildren of Jasper Petulengro are still of the Norfolk scene, part of the peoples drawn from Danish, Jutish, Dutch, Huguenot and Saxon blood, who make up our race of East Anglians.

You recollect Borrow's words, a picture as eloquent as Munnings's own pictures of his gipsy jockey, Page:

They are widely different in their appearance from the other people of the fair; not so much in dress, for they are clad something after the fashion of rustic jockeys, but in their look—no light brown hair have they, no ruddy cheeks, no blue quiet glances belong to them; their features are dark, their locks long, black, and shining, and their eyes are wild; they are admirable horsemen but they do not sit the saddle in the manner of common jockeys, they seem to float or hover upon it, like gulls upon the waves; two of them are mere striplings, but the third is a very tall man with a countenance heroically beautiful but wild, wild, wild.

It was to Borrow, standing on Castle Hill one day, when the gipsies and horse-dealers, the cattle-drovers and farmers were all a swirl of humanity beneath the tall white walls of Castle Blanch-flower, standing grim on its green hill where daffodils bloom in gold, that there came the greatest horse in all Norfolk, Old Marshland Shales, bred from a mare called Hue and Cry, who dropped her immortal foal in the archway beneath the altar of the magnificent church of Walpole St. Peter 140 years ago. Hue and Cry was of the old, old race of Norfolk pack-horses, whose like crossed the wild heaths and trod the long marshland dams centuries ago when Norfolk wool and worsted went to London Market by pack-train.

So whenever I stand upon Castle Hill I think of George Borrow's words in *Lavengro*:

So it came to pass that I stood upon this hill observing a fair of horses. . . . An old man draws nigh; he is mounted on a lean pony, and he leads by the bridle one of these animals; nothing very remarkable about that creature, unless in being smaller than the rest and gentle, which they are not; he is not the sightliest look; he is almost dun, and over one eye a thick film has gathered.[1]

But, stay, there is something remarkable about that horse; there is something in his action in which he differs from all the rest; as he advances, the clamour is hushed. All eyes are turned upon him. What looks of interest and respect and what is this? People are taking off their hats—surely not to that steed? Yes, verily! Men, especially old men, are taking off their hats to that one-eyed steed, and I hear more than one deep "Ah".

"What horse is that?" said I to a very old fellow, the counterpart of the old man on the pony, save that the last wore a faded suit of velveteen and this one was dressed in a white frock.

"The best in Mother England," said the very old man, taking a knobbed stick to his mouth and looking me in the face, at first carelessly but presently with something like interest.

"He is old, like myself, but can still trot his twenty miles an hour. You won't live long, my swain, talk and overgrown ones like these never does—yet if you

[1] The old horse was then thirty years of age. J.W.D.

should chance to reach my years you may boast to thy grandboys thou has seen Marshland Shales."

Amain I did for that horse what I would neither do for Earl or Baron—doffed my hat. Yes, I doffed my hat to the wondrous horse, the fast trotter, the best in Mother England and I, too, drew a deep "Ah!" and repeated the words of the old fellows around: "Such a horse as this we shall never see again; a pity that he is so old."

Borrow's vivid description of that scene on Castle Hill reminds us that Norwich is not merely a city of monks and bishops, of artists and merchants, nor solely a place where men make mustard and shoes, brew beer and manufacture great products in iron and steel, but that it is essentially, at heart, a city of the land. You may still see a drove of bullocks, a flock of sheep or a string of horses being driven through Norwich streets, hear the squealing of pigs being loaded into lorries and walk into inns where farmers and drovers, teamer-men and tractor drivers, thatchers and marshmen gather of ancient right.

The country is never far away. You smell it on the winds of spring and the sweet gales of autumn and at night under the stars, when the market stalls are shuttered and the bullock pens are empty, the factories are still and the lights are out, you may hear the wild geese chanting overhead, the wings of wild duck sibilant under the moon.

Chapter III

SOME OLD
NORWICH HOUSES

Strangers' Hall and Other Merchants' Dwellings

Quaker Memories

Tombland

III

DESPITE the outburst of muddled materialism in the 1930s, which resulted in the destruction of ancient beauty and the erection of the City Hall—each time I look at it I expect to hear railway wagons being shunted in its unlovely interior— Norwich preserves, by the good sense of its more educated citizens, past and present, a notable array of ancient houses and beautiful buildings.

Chief among them is the Strangers' Hall (18). If any man wished to walk into a house, old and welcoming, secret and full of treasures, that holds within its walls something of the best in the furnishings and homely tools of Englishmen throughout the last five centuries, he should walk into the Strangers' Hall. It lies near to the Maddermarket, in which is that most notable little theatre (24), a unique reconstruction of an Elizabethan playhouse which, under the direction of Mr. Nugent Monck, has become world-famous for its presentation of Shakespearian and other classical and period plays, as well as modern productions.

Strangers' Hall hides up an alley off Charing Cross. Much of it dates from the fourteenth century. It is a splendid specimen of a rich merchant's town house, built on the plan of a small country manor-house with a great hall, a fine old staircase, a musicians' gallery, a great deal of good panelling and the original stables. The rooms are furnished with meticulous care, to show English domestic life in reasonably prosperous households throughout the centuries.

There is an Elizabethan Room, a Carolean Room, an Anne Room, a Georgian Room and a Victorian Room. There is much good early Tudor furniture as well as Chippendale, Sheraton, Hepplewhite, marquetry and later Victorian mahogany. The collection of domestic and culinary utensils, wearing apparel, tools, fire-arms and personal knick-knacks is quite astonishing in its range, completeness and fidelity to the period. Everything is there, from pictures and pin-cushions to ball dresses, pottery, pistols, cooking-pots, lazy-tongs, velocipedes, riding-whips, spurs, fowling-pieces, spinets, spinning-wheels, early cradles, watchmen's rattles and man-traps for burglars. As a Folk Museum, it is easily one of the best in England. Unlike many such museums, it is neither overloaded nor are its rooms mere higgledy-piggledy collections of oddments. They are furnished as they would have been lived in. That is the great educational value and the intrinsic charm of this welcoming old house which, with its contents, was bequeathed to the city by the late Mr. L. G. Bolingbroke.

As for the rest of the ancient houses which make Norwich a place of recurring delight, there is, in King Street, the long, bland and gabled front of the old Musick House which, for centuries after Norman times, was always a Jew's house. Later, it became the property of the Pastons and of Lord Chief Justice Coke, but, after the First World War, it acquired a new effulgence, for there Mr. Nugent Monck's unmatched "Norwich Players" began that renaissance of the theatre in Norwich which so soon acquired world fame.

No one would accuse the General Post Office of architectural beauty or homely welcome, but it acquires second-hand importance from the fact that it stands where stood the old Griffin Inn, in which John Crome was born in 1768. It is a short bowshot—and I wonder how many people realise when they use that simile that a good archer can shoot an arrow more than a quarter of a mile—a short bowshot, then, to Tombland where sunlight through shifting leaves dapples the pebbled walks; newspapers are sold from kiosks in the open; old silver and good china beckons the connoisseur, sometimes at most fantastic prices; parsons and priests dart in and out of a most decorous ancient restaurant and coffee-place where they keep good furniture and hang good pictures on the wall; and, to cap it, the youth and beauty of Norwich go to dance in that ancient house guarded at its doorway by the mighty figures of Samson and Hercules.

Beside that enchanting little alley-way, which they call Tombland Alley(22), where is a most excellent bookshop, there lurches drunkenly the half-timbered front and leaning gable of an ancient

21   The Great Hospital, Norwich: the Master's House (*c.* 1450)

22   Tombland Alley, Norwich, showing the half-timbered house of Augustine Steward

23 The Octagon Chapel, Norwich (1756): the interior
Thomas Ivory, architect

24 The Maddermarket Theatre, Norwich, with its apron stage

Tudor house in which dwelt Augustine Steward, who, in his time, was mayor, sheriff and Member of Parliament. This old house, with its fine carving, its bay windows, stone steps and bland and mellow air, saw the bloodshed and heard the clash of arms when Kett's rebels stormed through the city and clapped Thomas Codde, the mayor, in jail. Through all that troubled time Augustine Steward, who lived in this ancient house, was deputy mayor of the city, a man distracted by civil war, riot, rape and pillaging.

If you leave Tombland and walk into the Cathedral Close(5), through that magnificent gate, which takes its name from Sir Thomas Erpingham, who commanded the rearguard at Agincourt, you pass into a place of ancient peace, of sunlit lawns, where hollyhocks bloom against sun-warmed walls of flint and pigeons coo and sparrows strut. There, on the left, is the old Charnel House Chapel of the vanished Priory. To-day it is part of the King Edward VI School, that most ancient public school, whose stars included Nelson and John Crome, George Borrow and Rajah Brooke, James Martineau and, in our own time, Sir Forrest Fulton and Sir Ernest Wild, both Recorders of London. Norwich Grammar School has had many distinguished headmasters and its standard of scholarship is as high now as at any time in its long history.

The Chapter House of the old monastic community has gone, but many of their buildings can still be traced, and the old water-gate, known to generations of Norwich folk as Pull's Ferry, is still a charming and peaceful riverside corner, but, alas, the Cow Tower, where the monks collected their dues from ships and boats passing up the river, is in a ruinous state. Indeed, one may say of Norwich Cathedral and its Close, as my good friend, R. H. Mottram, that shining light of Norfolk literature, has written: "Few of our Cathedrals and Closes show so clearly what must have been the plan and the independent jurisdiction of a pre-Reformation religious community."

In Tombland, if you follow Palace Street, there is much of the old Close wall, fortress-like in its solidity, and then you come to St. Martin-at-Palace Plain, where is a house with a plaque which tells you that here lived that outstanding painter of the Norwich

School, John Sell Cotman, which is hard by the fifteenth-century gateway to the Bishop's Palace.

This road leads on towards the ancient Bishop's Bridge over the Wensum, the bridge that was forced by Kett's rebels. But, before you reach the bridge, there lies on the left a plat of green grass with tall lupins and hollyhocks set brilliantly about it. There are flowers in a middle bed and round this oasis of grass and sunshine stand ancient almshouses, quiet and calm, like old ladies dozing in the sun, with a tall, quiet church, the church of St. Helen, keeping a motherly eye on them. This place of peace is known as the Great Hospital (7, 21), and it was endowed in 1249. There is a good roof in the chancel, the cloisters are a place of holy calm and there is an ancient cannon of Kett's time to remind you that once blood ran in Bishopgate and men were hurled, wounded and screaming, to drown in the river.

A good building of a different sort is the old Assembly House, which later became the Girls' High School, a wonderful example of domestic architecture now scheduled as an Ancient Monument. It was designed by Thomas Ivory, a local architect, about the middle of the eighteenth century, and is now the city's Art Centre.

Among other buildings, the Roman Catholic church of St. John, built by the late Duke of Norfolk on the site of the old city jail, is worth visiting, as is the old Bridewell, once the home of William Appleyard, who became the first mayor under the full Charter of 1403. It is a good fourteenth-century merchant's house, with a medieval prison in the crypt, a courtyard of Georgian period, and is now a Craft Museum.

In Church Alley, which is off Colegate, you will find a splendid fifteenth-century flint-built house once owned by a Quaker wine merchant named Sparswell, whose young son was a pupil of John Crome. The near-by church of St. Clement contains the grave of the parents of Matthew Parker, Archbishop of Canterbury, who, before he rose to the episcopal crown, walked into Kett's rebel camp at the risk of his life. Where Church Alley joins Colegate there stands another fine flint house, which was once the town house of the Prior of Ixworth, and next to it is a good merchant's house of the eighteenth century. Near by is the Old Meeting Place, handsomely built in 1693. The Rev. John Cromwell, cousin of the Lord Protector, was one-time Minister of its congregation.

Another fine flint-built merchant's house of an opulent sort is Bacon's House, which stands between Calvert Street and St. George Street, once called Gildengate. In this parish of St. George there was born, in 1752, Luke Hansard, who learnt the printing trade in Norwich, became official printer of the debates in the House of Commons and gave his name to the Hansard of to-day. In the parish there once stood, in Cross Street, the old Cow Cross, at which the city cow-herd gathered the citizens' cows, whilst Gilden-gate was said to have taken its name from the fact that herrings were kippered or "gilded" there.

Crome often drank his beer in "The Rifleman" public house, famous locally as "The Dirty Shirt Club".

Finally, among ancient buildings of note, is the twelfth-century Magdalen Chapel which, once the best-known leper house outside the city gates, is now preserved as the Lazar House Library.

Norwich is renowned for its narrow alleys or "lokes", which correspond somewhat to the "folleys" of old Colchester, the "courts" of fourteenth-century Kendal, or the "rows" of Yarmouth. Surely the narrowest is Jenkin Lane, a mere 2 feet 2 inches wide, which used to lead to the severely handsome Quaker Meeting House which, alas, was destroyed in 1942. Its green yard is full of the names of Gurneys and other famous Quakers who, from humble beginnings, rose to opulence as bankers and merchants. Magdalen Street can show a number of good eighteenth-century merchants' houses, in one of which, No. 10, Henry Thomas Martineau, the merchant, brought up those two later-famous children, Harriet and James. Harriet was born almost opposite in a house in Gurney's Court, where plaques inform the curious tourist that it was the home and original banking-house of John Gurney before he took his office to Bank Plain and set himself up as a country squire in Earlham Hall. That remarkable daughter of the Gurneys, Elizabeth Fry, was born in this house.

Other notable Norwich "lokes", leading off ancient Ber Street, are Mariners Lane and Southgate Lane, Stepping Lane and St. Julian's Alley. The latter takes its name from Dame Juliana

Berners, the fourteenth-century mystic and authoress of *Sixteen Revelations of Divine Love*. She was the first woman writer in the English tongue and, incidentally, quite an authority on falconry, hunting and the sports of the field.

Norwich owes much to the latter-day public spirit of the Colmans, the mustard kings, whose great works employ hundreds of citizens; to the Gurneys, who have provided many philanthropists and at least one outstanding naturalist, the late J. H. Gurney; and to others of its merchants and captains of industry who have brought trade and commerce to the city and, in their several ways, have helped preserve its ancient beauties and enhance its newer amenities.

Until the onset of the eighteenth century the Dukes of Norfolk were its overlords. Their great palace, the site of which is now a modern street, was built from the stones of the mighty Abbey of St. Benet-at-Holm, that little marshland principality which to-day is no more than a haunted field where cattle graze, herons fish and owls hoot from the few gaunt ruins that still stand bleakly magnificent.

As I have written elsewhere[1]: "That palace, for many years, was the feudal hub and centre of the city's life. The dukes lived there as little kings. Their state was magnificent, their generosity munificent, their retainers like unto an army, their entertainments princely.

Then came a day when the citizens of Norwich obstructed the Duke's will. They made churlish objections to a great pageant proposed. So the Duke razed his palace to the ground, and the stones of St. Benet's were scattered to the winds. Who knows but that to-day some humble dwelling-house in the back streets of the city is not builded of them, that some wall is not cornered with their fine quoins, or that the very street that you walk upon is not founded upon their buried remains? Thus the Dukes "cast their shoon" in the face of Norwich, and Norwich was none the better, for they were good overlords. There are some who say that this final demolishing of the palace was the fulfilment of that curse which follows all who build their houses from the sacred stones of churches.

[1] *Marshland Adventure*, Geo. Harrap & Co. Ltd., 1950.

Chapter
IV

BROADLAND
SCENE

From Norwich to Rockland Broad
Bitterns and Otters, Harriers and a "King"
On Birds and Fish and Ancient Peace

IV

CHARLES II thought nothing of the county of Norfolk. He described it as being fit only to be cut up in order to make roads for the rest of the country. Horace Walpole wrote shudderingly of "the wilds of Norfolk", and we all know that classic description of Holkham as a place so barren that "two rabbits might often be seen fighting for one blade of grass".

Now these are unseemly libels upon one of the fairest counties in all England, a county which not only is a place of blue skies, of that extraordinary blue, which is more than Mediterranean in its quality, for it has a freshness, a clean depth uniquely its own, but also a county which is the driest in England, a place of sunlit delight in summer and of sharp and bitter winds in winter. So much for the climate, which is a good one, being the best of both extremes.

As for the face of the county, no man wrote greater truth than old Thomas Fuller, when he said:

All England may be carved out of Norfolk, represented therein not only to the kind but degree thereof. Here are fens and heaths and light and deep and sand and clay ground and meadow and pasture and arable and woody, and [generally] woodless land, so grateful to this shire in the variety thereof. Thus, as in many men, though perchance this or that part may justly be cavilled at, yet all put together complete a proper person; so Norfolk collectively taken hath a sufficient result of pleasure and profit that being supplied in one part, which is defective in another.

There is a true picture. Norfolk has almost everything except mountains which produce rain and coal which breeds factories, Socialism and dirt.

Few counties in England have finer great houses or possess lovelier or more distinctive manor-houses, farmhouses and cottages. The great houses span almost all periods of architecture from the ornate Jacobean of Blickling to the massive Palladianism of Holkham to the uncomprising Norman keeps of Norwich Castle, Caister Castle and Castle Rising. Many of the houses, particularly the smaller ones, bear marked Dutch influence, which is especially noticeable in the crow-stepped gables, an everyday feature of farmhouse and cottage.

The country to the south and west of Norwich up the pleasant wooded valleys of the Yare(2) and the Wensum is charmingly pastoral—broad valleys with great woods standing massed on upland ridges, Georgian and Tudor mansions sitting blandly in rook-murmurous parks, little villages whose cottages are red-tiled or thatched straggling amiably by roadside heavy with the scent of beanfields, below uplands yellow with corn that reach those blue distances which the Norwich painters have immortalised.

Some of those villages, Costessey, for example, where stood until a few years since Lord Stafford's great mansion amidst embowering woods, are now being overrun by the suburban tentacles creeping out from Norwich. But, by and large, the immediate Norwich countryside is still lovely and unspoiled. There are unspoilt villages and pleasant halls set in green parks within a few miles of the city—at Keswick(26), that cradle of the Gurney family; at near-by Intwood, where Sir Thomas Gresham, founder of the Royal Exchange, lived in the old hall now incorporated in the larger house of the Unthank family; at Dunstan where Elizabethan and Queen Anne cottages cluster about a great common and the great house with its gables and quaint old chimney-stacks stand in a heavily wooded park.

There is another good hall at Ketteringham, a turreted and battlemented Tudor house, which has been the home of de Greys, Heveninghams, Atkyns, Boileaus, and is now a recent acquisition of the Duke of Westminster.

When the Huguenot Boileaus came to Ketteringham they brought with them a treasure which might well be the envy of the proudest museum or greatest castle in France—nothing less than the Sword of Bayard, the knight without fear and without reproach.

We may guess that this long, plain, undecorated sword is none other than the weapon which the hero flourished when, mortally wounded at the Battle of Sesia, he ordered his soldiers to set him facing the enemy with his back to a tree. It may well have been the

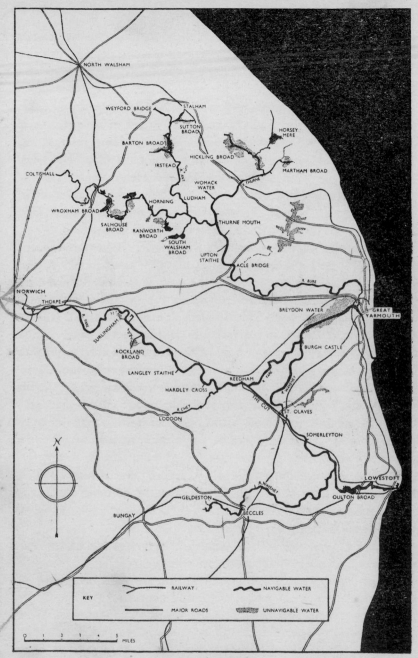

25 The Broads

sword with which single-handed he held the bridge against 200 Spaniards, the weapon which accompanied him when, with a garrison of only 1,000 men the great Chevalier held Mézières against an army of 35,000. There is a brass to Lady Jane Grey in the church, some old glass to the Grey family, other good brasses and the grave of Sir John Boileau, the great archaeologist who saved Burgh Castle, at the head of Breydon Water, the great Roman camp castle from destruction.

A little to the north within this easy perimeter of Norwich lies Colney Hall in a hilltop, within a lovely park at whose gates by the river clusters that most attractive village with its gabled cottages, the church with a round tower and the churchyard sloping to the green water-meadows starred gold with kingcups by the narrow winding river.

Nearer still to Norwich lies the great park of Crown Point Hall, the seat of the Colman family, and near by, in the tiny village of Arminghall, is probably the most remarkable historic relic in all Norfolk, if not indeed in England—an oak temple, 3,500 years old, around which Bronze Age chieftains lie buried in barrows. The existence of this unique "Woodhenge" was completely unknown until 1929, when odd markings on an aerial photograph showed eight black patches inside a broad ring like a horseshoe and a narrower outer ring led to excavations. The black patches were the spots where eight oak posts were set up, each 3 feet across and charred at the bottom to prevent rotting before being buried 7 feet deep. The outer circle has a diameter of 262 feet and the middle area is 87 feet across. Alas, this unique burial ground is now merely a field, a site, and no longer a temple.

The visitor to Norwich, however, naturally gravitates to the Broads rather than to the more orthodox rural country on the other sides of the city.

Below the park at Crown Point the Yare and Wensum meet, and there, if one takes a boat, say, from Thorpe, "the Richmond of Norwich", which Stannard made famous in his lively and luminous picture "Thorpe Water Frolic", the whole of Broadland lies waiting to be explored. There are more than 200 miles of waterways and over 5,000 acres of meres and lagoons in this flat, fascinating and unique survival of primitive England, which is called Broadland. It is, in plain fact, the tenuous survival, in isolated pools and meres, of the once wide and spreading waters of that vast, brackish, estuarine swamp and lagoon which the Romans called Gariensis.

To-day, the rivers which fed the great swamps and lost themselves in the shining bosom of the estuary are embanked. The marshes are drained. Dykes cross them like shining swords. Cattle graze where wild geese once nested. Suffolk Punches gallop clumsily over quaking levels where once the spoonbill stalked in white dignity, the bittern boomed on nights of spring and wildfowl filled the sky.

But they have never drained it all, nor embanked the last acre, nor canalised the last yard of open water. It is still a half-and-half land, half water and half land, half wild and half tame. Wind and water are still the lurking masters of the drained marshes and the low lands by the rivers. If there is a big tide and easterly gales in the North Sea, the salt water comes almost up to Norwich itself. Fish are drowned by the thousand sometimes 20 miles from the river mouth. If the drainage system which once descended upon the winds of heaven and is now largely the slave of electricity, that unreliable servant, were to break down for a week or even a few days of high December tides and easterly gales, half East Norfolk might well be drowned, a sea of glimmering waters as far as eye could reach.

Each winter the pounding threat of high tides, beating spumily against the weak sandhills at Horsey Gap, at Somerton Gap, at Waxham and elsewhere, is a constant and terrifying threat.

There have been many great inundations, the last as recently as 1937, when thousands of acres were flooded in the Horsey district, and the threat will continue. This is a land of unceasing battle.

The days of further drainage of the Broads fortunately have passed. Those which remain will be preserved. Those which, like parts of Barton Broad and the whole of Sutton Broad, have gradually grown up into a floating reedland, will gradually be deepened, cleaned out and restored to open water. For the Broads to-day are a natural asset, not only as an historic survival of a vanished past, or as unique sanctuaries of rare birds and uncommon plants, but as a national playground, an individual asset to the county of Norfolk.

Now the Yare(3), on which we set sail from this enchanting

village of Thorpe-next-Norwich, is broadest, deepest and, in its own way, loveliest of the Broadland rivers. To begin with, there are fewer boats upon it. It attracts less visitors than the northern rivers of Bure, Thurne and Ant. That means that in the bright months of summer we may sail in peace without too much of the doubtful company of the banjo boys and the head-scarf girls who, for two or three brief months, desport themselves in raucous gaiety never too far from the riverside inns of the more popular riverside villages. You will not find many of them on the Yare, for which the god of deep waters be praised. And there are even fewer on that enchanting river, the Waveney, which flows to the south through old, forgotten towns, red-roofed and drowsy in the sun, through water-meadows gold with kingcups and alive with springing snipe. There, indeed, is a river of peace.

Now, as you sail past the jumbled roofs, red-tiled and thatched, the flint-built cottages and sleepy waterside inns which, like the willows, dabble their toes in the water at Thorpe, you will see, away to the right, great massed woodlands, rising nobly against the sky. These are the woods about Crown Point Hall. And, at the foot of those woodlands, lies a sewage farm of note and renown. For, on that unsavoury waste, marked on the map as Whitlingham Sewage Farm, five guns on December 20th, 1927, shot no less than 230 snipe in one day. That, they say, is a record for England. It may well be. But what is even more surprising is the fact that it should have been made within less than a mile of the busy outskirts of Norwich.

A little farther on, the river bends to the right. On the left rises a little hill, bold for these flat parts, crowned with a great clump of firs which stand, wild and challenging, against the sky. That is Postwick which, hereabouts, they call "Possick". Below Postwick, leaving the rather pretty-pretty waterside hamlet of Bramerton Woods End on the right, you come, within a mile or so, to a flat and reedy waste of bog and waters which spreads away to the right into an African infinity of jungle mysteries. Nowhere is this mysterious jungle more than a mile long and little more than half a mile wide, but the dykes and waterways which thread sinuously through the tall reeds, reeds which rise 12 or 14 feet above the water, have all the air of leading one into a place of deadly mystery. In this ancient swamp, which is no more than the grown-up remains of what, some hundreds of years ago, was a great broad, there lies the shallow, forgotten little mere that is Surlingham Broad. Nowhere is Surlingham more than a few feet deep and, since the river-level rises and falls with the pull of the tides at Yarmouth, much of it, at times, is no more than a few inches deep. It is no place for any boat that will not sail in the track of a snail or in the dew upon the grass. For that reason you will probably have Surlingham Broad entirely to yourself. You may see there wild ducks spattering in the reeds, coots swimming in dignity, moorhens flicking their white tails with perky importance and, if you are lucky, you will hear on nights of spring and summer the ghostly booming of the bittern.

Once upon a time Surlingham Broad was famous for its fish. Charlie Gibbs, that ancient broadsman of Brundall, the village which lies on the other side of the river, is "King" of the Broad. It is only a few years since he took a 22-lb. pike out of the broads. Wherever there is a pike worth catching, Charlie is pretty sure to have it, as witness that $25\frac{1}{2}$ pounder, which you will see, stuffed in glassy majesty, in the bar of the Yare Hotel on Brundall waterside. Charlie Gibbs caught that in Ormesby Broad only a few years ago.

When Charlie was young, which is long years ago, a local bigwig tried to claim the broad as his private property. Charlie rose in his wrath as defender of the rights of the common man. He bought an old ship's boat in Yarmouth, anchored it on the broad and lived aboard in the tiny cabin for an entire winter, with his rod and gun and net, existing on what he caught and shot.

Charlie's version of the manner in which, single-handed, he conducted his war and won it, is illuminating and pungent. Setting his pint pot firmly down on the counter of the Yare Hotel one evening, beneath the glassy eye of his monster pike, he stroked his Viking moustache with a hand brown and seamed as leather and, fixing me with a benign blue eye, said: "I told 'em the broad allus had been public and I was goin' to stop there and see it stayed public. If they wanted to shift me they'd have to do it by force. Then I'd have the lot of them up before the magistrits! I told 'em I'd loaded me owd gun full o' swan-shot and that she was liable to go off on her own account if any b—— come nigh of my boat! They kept away all right!

"But, lor', what a winter I had. That snew. That fruz. That hailed. That rined! Some nights I was suffin' cold, I tell ye. But I stuck it even if me fitten [feet] felt as if they'd been frawned [frozen] off.

"I took stones on stones of eels and a masterful lot of big owd pike, and shot a few score of ducks, so, one way an' another, I didn't du too bad.

"Arter a year or two they give it up as a bad job and the gennleman what reckon'd he owned the broad told me, nice as pie, that I could fish there any time I liked, perwided I went up to the house and asked permission!

"So up I goos to the big house one night and told the gennleman, polite as you like, that he could have a *share* in the broad along wi' me an' the rest of the public.

"Then I invited him to come and have a day's fishin' with me and promised him that he'd have some rare good fish too. I told him I knowed where all the fish were and the big 'uns had got my mark on 'em—jest the same as the nick in the tail o' that big owd boy up in the glass case yinder.

"Well, the gennleman he laughed. He gives me a damn great whisky. Ha! three or fower on 'em!—and he says: 'All right, Gibbs, you win! We'll call it *our* broad in future. Now show me how to catch these private fish o' yourn.'

"Well, we parted good pals an' I took him out an' we soon had a tidy fish in the boat. He was happy an' so was I. But, lor', bless yer, that owd broad ain't half the place it was. That used to be thick wi' fish. Now it's thick wi' mud. What that broad needs is not so much argument but more dredgin'!"

The adventures of Charlie would, in a trite phrase, fill a book. Typical of the ancient race of broadsmen, he is a primitive man, a shooter and fisher by instinct, highly individual, sternly independent, with a simple, strict philosophy, an abiding sense of humour and no time for fools.

Fishing off Coldham Hall, that famous inn of anglers, which

stands, thatched and bold, on the bend of the river below Surlingham Broad and the red roofs of Brundall, he was witness, in 1939,
of a remarkable angling feat. A one-armed angler named Halliday
came there to fish. He was left-handed, but somehow he contrived
to put his live bait on the hook single-handed and fish single-
handed. And, lo! he hooked a 36-lb. pike, played it and landed it
without any help whatsoever. As Charlie succinctly put it: "If that
ain't a record, it damn well ought to be."

Below Brundall the river valley opens into a wide, marshland
vista. Acres upon acres of reed and sedge sigh in the wind and
ripple in sunlight like the waves of a green sea. Reed warblers
chitter their endless tiny songs. Sometimes the marsh harrier or
Montagu's harrier beats the lonely level like a setter—flap and glide,
flap and glide—and then an airy swing with the ease of an eagle.
Wild duck pass over on quick wing or quack softly in hidden
dykes. Water-rails squeal suddenly like stuck pigs in green jungles.
The bittern creeps, a brown gnome, through secret runways in the
reeds or takes to wing, flapping, brown and moth-like, above ancient
morasses that knew his kind a thousand years ago. Overhead peewits
weep and wail and stumble in airy acrobatics. From the river's
edge the heron, grey-blue and ghostly as a shadow, lumbers up on
huge wings and flaps like a blown rag into the far flat distances that
run on to the salt tides of Breydon and the beckoning of the outer
sea. It is an ancient and unspoilt valley of great skyscapes and green
and brown landscapes where clouds sail like huge galleon. By
night the grasshopper warbler, the "reeler" bird of the old fenmen,
reels his endless thin song in the brooding silences.

To the right, a great green sea of marshes, choked with reeds and
sedge, with here and there an island of sallow bushes or hairy
willows standing up, runs on into the distance to the wild and lonely
broad of Rockland and the empty uplands beyond, where distant
ploughlands crown the low horizon. On the left are rough cattle
marshes dotted with herds of grazing Friesians. Windmills stand
sentinel at the end of dykes where teal whistle and moorhens patter
about their business. At the marsh edge a long fringe of ancient
woodland runs parallel with the river for half a mile or so. Those
are the woods of Strumpshaw Hall, where for many years lived

that good old sportsman and excellent naturalist, the late Squire Holmes.

Charlie Gibbs tells of how, fifty years ago, he caught a marsh harrier in a trap and took it to the squire, who gave him a sovereign for it and, for years after, kept it alive as a pet.

A little farther down the river there is a broad dyke which strikes straight and blue as a sword-blade into the heart of the reed fens. It is about half a mile long, broad and deep. If you sail up it you will come suddenly to the shining, lonely waters of Rockland. Almost the least spoiled of all the broads, it is, to my mind, the broad which most nearly preserves the true character and appearance of the old, vanished fenland meres of Cambridgeshire and Lincolnshire. As you sail on to it out of the dyke, there in front lie the lonely shining waters of the broad. One or two small islands of reeds, where coots and crested grebes nest, stand up. To the left are a few scattered, wind-blown willows. At the foot of the nearest one to the dyke-mouth you are almost certain to find the "spraint" of an otter, the fish-scales and bones of his last breakfast. For the roots of that old tree for long years have been an "otter's altar". To the right the broad spreads to a far, low shore of reeds and sedge. Somewhere amid those reed-beds a narrow channel goes winding through quaking swamps where the great South American marsh-rat or nutria, bigger than an otter, has his home, to the tiny hidden pool which is Wheatfen Broad, the private preserve of that excellent naturalist, Dr. E. A. Ellis. The great clump of thorns and willows and mixed trees looming above the reed-beds behind Wheatfen holds a heronry. The heron is the daily familiar of these wet wastes and windy skies—the bird in whose shadowy ghostliness is typified something of the mystery, the grace and the aerial beauty of the broadland waters and skies.

Sit idly in a boat, hidden among the reeds, on the edge of Rockland on a day in spring and you will see terns dipping and flashing above the sun-shot waters. Black-headed gulls laugh above the tasselled reeds. Swans, majestically priggish, float in flotillas of a dozen or more, the enemies of young ducklings whom they seize and drown with ruthless ferocity.

There are mallard preening themselves in a reedy bay; pochard,

26 Keswick, Norfolk, on the River Yare. The church has been in ruins since early in the seventeenth century

27 "Old Scientific" Fuller, the famous fowler of Rockland Broad

28 Removing the catch at Rockland, Norfolk

Eel Picking

84

red-headed and plump as butter-balls, asleep on the edge of a glistening mud bank where redshank flit to and fro and ring their springtime bells of song.

Sometimes a passing shadow sends the moorhens scuttling for cover as a harrier sweeps over in a half-mile glide with the ease of an eagle. Solitary and unperturbed, the great-crested grebe, shining cream and chestnut in the sunlight, his ear-tufts proudly erect, dives in the centre of the broad and, seemingly minutes later, bobs up 150 feet away.

The courtship of the grebes alone is a thing of pure delight. They swim towards each other, bowing and nodding in the most cavalierly fashion and then, beak to beak, rise on their paddles, rub their breasts together and, one would almost swear, kiss each other.

At night, when the broad is still and silent, the dull, thumping boom of the bittern throbs through the fenland silence. The thin whistle of the otter, like the whistle of a train, far distant and faint, cuts the silence, a knife-edge of sound. That round, bullet-like shape, cleaving a V of dark ripples across the moonlit water, is the mother otter on her way to feed her kittens amid the tangled roots of an ancient willow. The harsh "fraa-aank" of a heron, the "harnser" of the marshmen, is the haunting ghostly note that dominates the scene by night and day.

Rockland is no more than 120 acres of water, but the flatness and wide expanse of the surrounding reedland and the green cattle marshes of Claxton give it an air and atmosphere of immensity. Rockland village, what little there is of it, lies at the head of Rockland Dyke, a broad, quiet waterway leading from the far side of the broad through sedgy wildernesses of sallow bushes and creamy meadow-sweet until it ends in a sprawl of old thatched cottages, chicken-runs and stranded boats.

Years ago Rockland was the home and kingdom of that remarkable old broadsman, the late "Scientific" Fuller(27), the self-styled and universally acknowledged "King of Rockland Broad"(28). Like Charlie Gibbs at Surlingham, he stoutly upheld the public right to shoot and fish unhindered on Rockland Broad which, being tidal, is a right unchallengeable.

"Scientific" lived in an old houseboat on the broad. There he dwelt with his gun-punt and his great muzzle-loading punt-gun, his shoulder-guns and bow-nets, his eel spears and his dog. Short and broad-shouldered, with a great barrel of a chest, "stuggy", as they say in Norfolk, his eyes gleamed fiercely from a great black bush of beard, whiskers and unkempt hair. He feared neither man nor devil, and he was a master fisherman, a crack shot.

"Scientific" could skate at full speed across the broad, travelling at express speed with his gun in his hand, suddenly throw the gun to his shoulder and shoot, stone-dead, a gull wheeling and swooping overhead.

He caught an immense number of fish, shot thousands of wild-fowl and, in his time, collected many rare birds for wealthy collectors when such reprehensible practices were winked at. I shudder to think how many bitterns, bearded tits, harriers, rare warblers and uncommon ducks went into the great, bloodstained, canvas "side-bag" which swung on a broad strap from his shoulders.

This uncouth, lovable, pugnacious old man would swallow incredible quantities of beer at the inn which stands at the head of Rockland Dyke, and then, rattling his hob-nailed, leather water-boots on the stone floor, he would dance a wild jig which struck sparks from the flags and end up by challenging any man there to fight him for a quart. None did unless they were very young or very drunk.

In winter, when the punt-guns boomed through the snowy mist far away on the tidal flats of Breydon Water, "Scientific" would be afloat in his little, low, grey-painted duck-punt, the great muzzle-loader, with its barrel 6 feet long, lying flat and menacing in its cradle. A few minutes after the booming echoes sounded from Breydon, teams of duck and widgeon with sometimes skeins of grey geese would whistle overhead and plunge in sheets of foam on to the surface of the broad.

Like a shadow the old man's punt crept silently out of its little bay among the reeds and floated flat and ghostly towards the resting fowl. Foot by foot he spritted or paddled silently forward. Then the trigger was pulled. There came a red, searing flame, a foot long, from the muzzle, a billowing cloud of grey smoke, a thudding boom that echoed across the lonely fen and, in a frenzy of wings, the fowl were up and away, skirling with fright. On the water floated a dozen, perhaps a score, of dead and wounded. That was the old man's harvest in winter.

In summer he caught and netted fish, speared eels and took them in his great funnel-shaped "grigs" woven by hand from thin osiers.

If anyone poached on "Scientific's" preserves, he would shoot at them as soon as look at them. Yet he was universally loved, a sort of uncouth cross between "Bloody Morgan" and Thoreau. When he died half Norfolk mourned him and men of science who had enjoyed his company and bought his rare specimens knew that a last link with the primitive race of broadsmen had gone for ever.

To-day, a young, stolid, Saxon-looking, beefy-faced broadsman named "Fudgey" Stone, a famous marshland name, treads in the footsteps of "Scientific". He, too, shoots for a living and fishes for profit, but "Fudgey" is an archangel of innocence compared with the rip-roaring rumbustiousness of old "Scientific".

The opening day of the shooting season on Rockland nowadays is not merely dangerous for ducks but deadly for human beings. Guns are discharged from every reed-bed the instant the greenish dawn lightens the eastern skyline. Charges of shot whistle through the reeds. Pellets patter like red-hot rain into the water. One man I know, who had the innocent confidence to anchor half a dozen wooden decoy ducks in front of his hide, suddenly saw the whole lot riddled with shot and capsized in front of him by a double dis-charge from a hidden gun. Rockland, on the opening day of the shooting season, is no place for any visitor unless he is clad in chain-mail and has his head in a barrel.

I like that idyllic picture of Rockland as it was in the golden peace of Victorian England, when that earliest and most charming of Broadland chroniclers, the late Christopher Davies, sailed the Broads and wrote his prose pictures of what was then an unspoiled land of reeds and waters, untroubled by motor-boats, innocent of banjos and gramophones, free of scantily clad summer beauties from Leeds and Wigan, a place, in fine, of ancient peace. Christopher Davies wrote in 1883:

You are now in the haunt of heron and fowl and the silence is only broken by the bleating of snipes in the clear air above you. As far as poor humanity is concerned there is a floating palace and there are its king and its queen. True, the palace is but a large old sea-boat, with a hut built up in the centre third of it and roofed with planks and tarred felt; but within, all is neat and snug, and spacious enough for the wants of its occupants. And he who sits mending his nets is more free than any monarch. His gun and his nets bring him enough for his needs, his house is his own, his time is his own, he calls no man master, and he pays neither rent nor taxes. What more could you have? His wife is cleaning her crockery, and it is evident that she knows not the need or worry of a servant. Verily, the sobriety of advancing years and the cares of paternity do not prevent me from indulging in a dream of how free and idyllic such a life would be if one could take it, together with an educated love of nature, a stomach for dirty work—such as hauling in that long eel-net, which is now hung out to dry along the top of the boat. Between a couple of poles on the rond (which is very soft and wet) a casting-net is drying in the wind. Alongside the larger craft is a gunning-punt, with a couple of single-barrelled guns lying ready loaded in it. A few yards away is a group of gloating boxes or trunks, perforated with holes, in which the eels, tench, pike and other fish are kept alive until there are sufficient to send to Billingsgate.

The whole establishment is moored in a little reedy bay close by the mouth of the dyke.

Presently the man looks up. His keen eye has detected something moving at the far side of the lake. He gets into his punt, and sculls it with one oar worked in a side rowlock in a singular and rather inexplicable way, with great rapidity, and noiselessly. Skirting the reeds, and keeping as much as possible within the shelter of the straggling fringe of them which has advanced beyond the main body, he nears the spot where he has marked his quarry. The sun gleams on the barrel of his gun, there is a puff of white smoke, and the report comes loudly over the water, and he has picked up a coot, with which he returns to his hut.

He is a human spider. The Broad is his web; and when anything eatable touches it, he sallies out of his cell bent on destruction. Day and night he follows his pursuit; and though there are two or three others of his kind on the Broad, yet it is naturally a place so favourable in all its conditions to bird-life, that he says there is no diminution of fish or fowl attributable to his pursuits.

Indeed I take it that two or three amateur sportsmen spending a day on the water would, by their noise and racket about, do far more to frighten fowl away than he with all his slaughter; for he goes to work so unobtrusively, that only the fowl and fish which are killed find out how dangerous he is—(this last phrase sounds rather Irish, but let it pass).

His pursuits vary a little with the seasons, and this is the course of them. In the spring, when netting for roach and bream is forbidden, he keeps a good look-out for rare birds' nests and eggs, which find a ready sale among the many collectors in Norfolk. Perchance he finds some nests of the bearded tit, with their delicate little eggs, or he notes the nests of the heron, of which there are several scattered colonies about the Broads, and one small heronry close by, at Surlingham. If he does not take the eggs, he waits until the young birds are nearly able to fly, and then secures them alive. Occasionally, too, he shoots an otter, which are plentiful enough on the Broads, making their "hovers" in a beaver-like nest among the reeds.

In the summer he goes eel-picking (27, 28) or spearing, or bobbing for eels at night with a ball of worms strung on worsted, by which means he takes large quantities. Then, when the tench sun themselves in the shallow water on hot still days, he "tickles" them, absolutely lifting them out of the water with his hands. The silly fish simply hide their heads in the weeds when they are disturbed, and ostrich-like, imagine they are safe.

With the 1st of August the wildfowl season opens and then for a day or two Rockland Broad becomes populous with visitors. Before midnight on the last day of July, gentle and simple, professional and amateur, come in boats and take up their position, waiting patiently until the dawn brings flight-time, when some lucky ones will get seven or eight ducks before the flight is over. After that, the coots and water-hens find the day an unlucky one for them. The whizzing of shot about the Broad makes a nervous man feel uncomfortable. After the opening of the season, however, the professional has it pretty much his own way. In October the eels begin to move towards the estuary, and the eel-net is set across the dyke to catch them in its long "poke" as they pour off the Broad.

Eel-picking is an art in which some men attain considerable skill. They move gently along in their boats until they see the "blowing" of an eel, as the bubbles issuing from the mud are termed, and then they strike where the bubbles come from. They can distinguish between the blowing of a large or small eel and tell both from the blowing of a tench. They do not often strike at random. A still, fine day, during hot weather, is the most suitable time for this sort of work. On such days the wherrymen seize the opportunity when their vessel nears the bank to plunge the spears into the mud and so get a good many eels. The strokes of the spear are called "jowles". Sometimes an eel-picking match takes place on the Broad, between two rival champions, under conditions such as the following: The match to be finished in two hours; each man to have thirty jowles, each time calling out, "Here's a go!" first lifting the spear in the air to show that it is clear of eels, then making one stroke and then lifting the spear clean out of the water. The stakes are a sovereign aside, and the match to be decided by numbers, not weight. Each picker has in his boat a mate of his rival's to see fair play, and a boat with two referees in it accompanies the match.

Hanging up to dry by the eel-hut, you will see numerous bundles of reeds, each the size of a rolling-pin, and tightly and neatly tied up. These are the Broadman's "liggers", or trimmers, which he sets for pike all over the Broad. The line is rolled round the ligger with a foot or two free, and the double hook is baited with a roach. These are often set in water not a foot deep and really do not seem to do much harm to angling. The pike are too numerous at present and hence are very small. A friend of the writer's caught thirty with a spoon-bait one day in the river close by, nineteen of which had to be put back again.

The liggering on Rockland, therefore, does not interfere with the pike-fishing in the river. There is too great a craze in Norfolk just now for preserving. The consequence is that the rivers are overstocked; and the fish run short of food and are necessarily small. People complain that they catch no large fish now as they used to do in the old days before netting in the river was abolished but that they catch numbers of fingerlings. They have not yet learned that either you must have a medium stock of fish and large ones, or a teeming stock and small ones.

Rockland has changed little since Christopher Davies wrote those words. It is still the same wild, enchanting place. But when one has left Rockland there are no other broads on the lower reaches of the Yare with the exception of two small, private broads at Buckenham and Hassingham, both of which are owned and strictly preserved by my friend Mr. Holt-Wilson, and his brother. Rare birds are sure of a sanctuary there. Both broads are land-locked and therefore cannot be reached from the river.

29 South Walsham's two churches in one churchyard

Chapter
V

TO THE WATERS
OF WAVENEY

The Isle of Lothingland
A Lake of Monsters
Geldeston Lock and Oulton Broad
Wildfowl on Breydon
The Grandeur and the Ghosts of Burgh Castle

30 Oulton Broad, Lowestoft, Suffolk

31 Fritton Lake, Suffolk—one of the last working duck decoys is on it

32 Burgh Castle, Suffolk, from the air. The original Roman fortifications were begun in A.D. 47

V

BELOW Buckenham, where there is a good, solid, unpretentious inn on the river bank, a broad dyke on the right skirts a marshland carr of oaks, elms and willows and leads you to Langley Abbey. It is no more than a substantial farmhouse, but embodies considerable remains of the original Praemonstratensian abbey built by Sir Robert Fitzroger Helke in 1198. The abbey remains include a crypt, a spiral staircase, one or two very good arches and part of a moat.

It forms part of the Langley Park estate of some 7,000 acres or more. The hall, a large eighteenth-century building, is now a boys' school in a park of 800 acres, and the church is fourteenth century, rather barn-like, with a three-decker pulpit, a number of horsebox pews and a 600-year-old font. Some of the stained glass was brought from Rouen Cathedral at the time of the French Revolution.

Below Langley the scenery becomes almost completely flat, dominated for miles by the hideous bulk of the Cantley sugar-beet factory. Reedham, a mile or so lower down, is a charming riverside village, once the seat of Saxon kings and notable to-day for the fact that it possesses the last chain ferry in Norfolk. There is a heronry in an ancient wood on the Reedham marshes, a wood in which cormorants and spoonbills nested when Sir Thomas Browne was writing his enchanting descriptions of Norfolk bird life.

Below Reedham bridge a long canal, straight and glittering as a sword blade, cuts through the flat, green cattle marshes to the right. This is the New Cut, dug by Sir Morton Peto in about 1830. It connects the Yare with the River Waveney, to my mind the loveliest of all Norfolk rivers. If one sails up the New Cut you come to St. Olaves, small and charming, nestling by the waterside at the foot of the low, fir-crowned, sandy range of the Herringfleet Hills. This is the ancient Isle of Lothingland, no longer an isle but a place of unspoilt beauty. Most of the isle is on the 6,000-acre estate of

Somerleyton Hall, the property of Lord Somerleyton. It includes Fritton Lake(31), a land-locked sheet of water nearly a mile long, almost entirely surrounded by deep woodlands, at one end of which the Fritton duck decoy is still worked. Many of the ducks in the London parks have been caught in the Fritton decoy pipes, which regularly supplies London with its ornamental waterfowl.

Fritton Lake is, without doubt, the remnant of a deep salt-water estuary which, in Roman times, was an offshoot of the great bay of Gariensis.

Many rare birds have been recorded from Fritton, including bitterns, gadwall, garganey, peregrines and, within recent years, an osprey, which haunted the lake for weeks on end.

Boats can be hired from Mr. W. W. Ward of Fritton Old Hall Hotel, a mighty angler with some of the best pike-fishing in England on his doorstep. Some idea of the capabilities of Fritton as a home of monsters can be gathered from the fact that a sporting parson, the Reverend Mr. Stevens, fishing from the Old Hall lawn in the winter of 1947, caught one 25½-pounder, one 25-pounder, three 24-pounders and ten 16-pounders, *all in one day!*

To cap that incredible performance, there is the true tale of two local farmers, Mr. Skoulding and Mr. Noel, who caught thirty-nine pike, totalling 293 pounds, *in three hours*. Mr. Ward tells me that a few winters ago he and some of his guests caught 443 pike, all of them over 15 pounds in weight, fishing from his lawn, in seven weeks from December to February. During the same winter they returned no less than 936 fish under 15 pounds each. Those were the tiddlers!

One can navigate the waters of Waveney from St. Olave's south-wards, with the wooded little Herringfleet Hills on the left and the great, flat, green stretch of the Wheatacre Marshes on the right until you come to Oulton Dyke. There you leave the river, sail through a short stretch of marshes and come suddenly upon the shining bosom of Oulton Broad, where Borrow dwelt in his gaunt house, sang his gipsy songs at midnight, entertained his Romany friends and wrote *Lavengro* and *The Bible in Spain* in the old wooden octagonal summer-house which still stands "on the very margin of the water" beneath its moaning firs.

Alas, Oulton has lost much of its ancient peace and Victorian charm since Borrow's day, and I doubt much if he or Nicholas Everitt, that robust broadland squire, lawyer, author and sportsman who also dwelt upon its shores, would recognise much of it in these latter motor-boat days(30).

Everitt, who wrote that charming book *Broadland Sport*, which is now something of a classic, always said, in the days of my youth, that if you were to dig up a square foot of soil on Whitecast, which is a little marsh on the edge of the broad, you could sift at least an ounce of snipe shot from it. Snipe swarmed in his day, and this was their favourite spot whereon, winter after winter, ardent snipe-shooters discharged their fowling-pieces throughout the season. It was always said that you could, on a good day, see "from 500 to 1,000 snipe on the wing at the same time". The whole marsh is not more than 40 acres in extent, belongs to the parish and is, or was, always let to one person for the year. Even to-day, snipe still visit the broad in fair numbers, especially with an east wind in November or during a hard frost. However, no one is ever likely to see 500 on the wing at one time again, although, to be sure, two summers ago, I saw a bittern rise from a reed-bed opposite Borrow's house and fly, with the utmost unconcern, over a whole flotilla of yachts and motor-boats, which were taking part in an extremely noisy regatta.

Nowadays, Oulton is a busy, boat-building centre, with a public park named after "Nick" Everitt, a good hotel called "The Wherry", which has an entrancing collection of local otters, fish and fowl, and it is, of course, the backdoor to Lowestoft.

Lowestoft is a nice old town if you want to buy fish, ride a donkey on the sands, lunch or dine in the excellent Yacht Club-house or merely watch the drifters coming in and out of harbour. It has charm enough, though of no great architectural distinction, but one can hardly regard it as anything more than the extreme southerly gateway to the Broads, a place indeed from which it is better to set sail for the waters of Waveney rather than make it a base for the northern Broads.

Now the Waveney is, in many ways, the loveliest of all Broadland rivers. To begin with, it possesses no broads other than a land-locked, hidden little pool called Barnby Broad, which is private and full of ducks, but it winds its gentle and glancing course through scenery of the pastoral type that Sir Arnesby Brown has painted with such fidelity.

From its junction with Oulton Dyke it flows calmly for seven or eight miles through marshes bright with irises, gay with buttercups, dappled with cattle and musical with redshanks and peewits. Then the marshland scene contracts(31), low wooded uplands march nearer to the river and Beccles(33), that ancient town of Victorian peace and Georgian houses, steps graciously in long gardens to the riverside.

A little beyond Beccles there stands above the marshes that small and exquisite Tudor mansion, Roos Hall(34). With its narrow red bricks, its gracious proportions, mullioned windows and crow-stepped gables, it is the perfect miniature Great House. Luckily it is well lived-in and well cared for. Alas, the near-by Barsham Hall, that ancient, moated nursery of the Sucklings is, I hear, demolished. In the Jacobean rectory was born Catherine Suckling, the mother of Nelson. She married Edmund Nelson in St. Michael's Church at Beccles. In Barsham Church there is a memorial to a mighty knight, Sir Robert Atte Tye who, after he had made his fourteenth-century will, raised himself on his death-bed and, with his last breath, said: "I command that you, my friends and children, shall drink four dozen bottles of wine over my coffin before the earth is thrown upon it". On which commendable gesture he expired.

Beyond Roos Hall the river takes a bend through rich and reedy marshes, lively with snipe, where cattle and Suffolk Punches move slowly in the sun, and there ahead of you lies Geldeston Lock. It is a place of green peace. Its timbers are rotting and mossy. The little Lock Inn, demure and whitewashed, stands shyly on an island of willows with a reed-fringed garden about it.

Altogether, it has an early Victorian quality of the most seductive sort. A hundred years ago it was a favourite place for illegal prize-fights, since it had the unique advantage that the approach of police could be readily seen. Thereupon the combatants crossed the river from Norfolk into Suffolk, where they were safe, or from Suffolk into Norfolk if the Suffolk police were on their tracks.

Beyond the lock one cannot go in a boat of any size, so you must

33 Beccles, Suffolk: the fifteenth-century church, with its detached bell tower, seen across the River Waveney

34 Roos Hall, Beccles, Suffolk: a sixteenth-century
Manor House

35 Horstead Mill, near Coltishall, Norfolk. The timber water-mill is on the
River Bure

turn about and sail down-river to where Yare and Waveney unite below St. Olaves in the salt-water estuary of Breydon (42), the largest "lake" in Norfolk. It is about four miles long, three-quarters of a mile wide and covers about 1,200 acres. At low tide three-quarters of it are glittering mudflats. The channel across Breydon is marked by a series of huge posts and the incautious sailor who departs from the deep-water channel will very soon find himself stranded on the mud.

Dominating Breydon at the western end, where Yare and Waveney mingle their fresh waters with the salt, stand the gaunt and massive remains of Burgh Castle (32), the largest walled camp-castle in Britain. Its walls are 15 feet thick at the base and 15 feet in height, enclosing a space of some 6 acres of land, which is 640 feet long and 413 feet wide. Burgh was built in about the year A.D. 100, and it is generally held that the Roman general, Publius Ostorius Scapula, was its architect and builder.

Writing of it in *Broadland Adventure*, I said:

In Roman times we may imagine it as a walled village in which were houses for officers, barracks for men, stables for horses, kitchens and forges, armourers' shops and blacksmiths' furnaces, food stores and arsenals. A place of constant life, discipline and eternal watchfulness. The walls probably were never higher than they are to-day, but they were almost certainly surmounted by wooded palisades from behind which the archers could shoot. On the top of each bastion or tower was mounted a great ballista or catapult which could cast huge round stones upon the attackers whilst the archers, spearmen and javelin-throwers rained their lesser but deadlier missiles upon the skin-clad, hairy hordes of Britons from the reed-beds and marshes.

The late Mr. Harrod, the eminent archaeologist, who excavated at Burgh in 1850 and 1855, found traces of a western wall at least two hundred feet long. He also found oak piles which had been driven into the marshy ground on the west and remains of two guard-houses which had existed on either side of the main gateway which was in the centre of the east wall. That gateway was only eleven feet eight inches wide, just the width for a chariot to pass through. To-day it is a mere gap in the walls. Two other posterns, each five feet wide, can be traced in the centre of the north and south wall. Mr. Harrod also found remains of what probably was a bath house, sixteen and a half feet square.

This outstanding relic of the Roman occupation would have been almost entirely destroyed in the middle of the last century had not that good Norfolk squire, the late Sir John Boileau, Bart., of Ketteringham Park, stepped in and bought it. It is now safe for all time under the care of the Ministry of Works.

Today, Burgh Castle is a place of ghosts. Stand within its grey and glimmering walls on a summer night or under the chill moon of winter when the owls call, the curlew whistle like spectres on the mudflats, and the otter moves stealthily in the reeds and it is easy to imagine the stir and hum of the Roman camp, the clink of armour, the stamp and snuffle of war-horses, to see the dancing flicker of camp fires and to hear the lusty Roman choruses sung by men who had campaigned under every moon in Europe from the Tiber to the far, grey rampart of Hadrian's Wall.

Immediately below Burgh Castle, at the mouth of the Yare, lies the tiny marshland settlement known as Berney Arms. It consists of a public house without a licence, a farmhouse, a railway station and a few scattered cottages. There is no road to it other than a green grass track across the vast prairie of cattle marshes which stretch for miles inland until they reach the low uplands at Acle, eight or nine miles to the west. Berney Arms is dominated by the lofty tower of what is probably the tallest drainage mill in Broadland. In winter the inhabitants of this remote settlement are completely cut off from all communication with the outside world except by water or rail. Sometimes when the surrounding marshes are half flooded with shallow winter waters the scene is one of almost unspeakable desolation.

The marshes are visited in winter by thousands of wild geese and at one time were famous for snipe. Breydon is a wonderful home of wildfowl and waders and many rare birds turn up there on migration. It is one of the few places on the British coast where spoonbills are more or less regular annual visitors. Black terns are not uncommon on migration, whilst at times thousands of widgeon and other duck visit the estuary. Many of the rarest wildfowl on the British list have been recorded from Breydon. Probably the best collection of Breydon birds can be seen in the Dyke Road Museum at Brighton. They were collected by the late R. Fielding Harmer, a noted "gentleman gunner", who regularly punted on Breydon some sixty years or more ago. The collection is quite outstanding.

Chapter
VI

YARMOUTH AND
THE NORTH BROADS

The Trinity Broads
Hickling and Horsey Mere
Rare Birds and Sea Villages
St. Benet's Abbey and the Ranworth Missal
Salhouse to Horstead Mill

36   Reeds and Wildfowl on Ranworth Broad, Norfolk

37   Chapmans Mill on Hickling Broad, once the studio of Mr. Roland Green,
the bird artist

39   Herringfleet Marsh,
Suffolk: a drainage mill

VI

YARMOUTH catches fish, sells fish, thinks fish and smells fish. It has a sea-front several miles long, one of the finest quays in Europe, seats for 25,000 people on its front, and is proud of the fact that it was a seaport before the Normans came to England. Charles Dickens knew and loved Yarmouth. Nelson paid it visits. The Nelson monument near the sea-front is one of Yarmouth's proudest possessions, but its chief glory was the great parish church built during the reign of King John. It is in the shape of a cross, some 236 feet in length, 112 feet wide; but alas, it was gutted during the war. There was a little good German stained glass and once upon a time the church possessed no less than thirty chapels which were destroyed at the Reformation. Cromwell's friend, John Carter, and Cromwell's grand-daughter, Bridget Bendish, are both buried in the church.

Many of the rows, the narrow alley-ways of fishermen's cottages, so narrow that one can touch either wall when walking down them, were destroyed by bombing during the war, but enough are left to give one an idea of what old Yarmouth was like. They are not particularly attractive, architecturally or otherwise, and were, in all too many cases, breeding-grounds of vice, disease and unsanitary conditions.

The Fishermen's Hospital, erected in 1702, is picturesque and worth visiting, but the outstanding building in Yarmouth is the old Tolhouse, one of the most ancient municipal buildings in England. It was standing in 1362, but was much damaged in the late war. There was a good Early English doorway, a finely timbered roof in the hall and some forbidding dungeons in which prisoners were immured. Some remnants exist of the old Town Wall of Yarmouth, including King Henry's Tower and other fortifications, of which the North West Tower is a good example.

The Star Hotel is an outstanding piece of good Elizabethan

architecture, quite one of the most attractive buildings in the town.

From Yarmouth one sails up the Bure or north river, which connects in due course with the Thurne and the Ant, leading to the great range of the northern Broads.

The scenery from Yarmouth past Stokesby, Runham and Acle is flat marshland, most of it down to grass with, hidden among the low uplands on the right, the tower and moat of Caister Castle (38), the old seat of the Fastolfs and Pastons. Little remains other than the tower and some of the walls; an empty shell. It was built by Sir John Fastolf, who led the English archers at Agincourt, was present at the taking of Caen, was Governor of the Bastille and had the mortification of seeing his army put to flight by Joan of Arc.

After his death it went to the Pastons and endured the year-long siege by Thomas Mowbray, Duke of Norfolk, which is told at length in the Paston Letters. To-day, flowers bloom in the ruined walls, jackdaws nest in the empty tower and the waters of the moat reflect the grey stones that are part of English history.

At Acle, where there is a most excellent ancient inn, "The Bridge", full of good old furniture, prints, pictures and cottage antiques, one should take to the road and visit the near-by Trinity Broads, as Filby Broad, Rollesby Broad and Ormesby Broad are known. These are practically land-locked as the narrow Muck Fleet, which connects them with the River Bure, is impassable in anything except a duck-punt. The broads are singularly beautiful with much woodland on their shores, full of fish, the home of many wildfowl and rare birds, and populated by more crested grebes than I have seen anywhere else in Britain. One day I counted no less than seventeen of them, fishing and diving, from the bridge which spans the narrow neck of water that connects Filby Broad with Rollesby Broad. Boats can be hired on these broads and, owing to their inaccessibility, they are fortunately not over-populated with motor-cruisers, as are so many other broads, through being unnavigable.

Some three miles above Acle Bridge the River Thurne, broad and deep, leads through the flat marshes on the right to Potter Heigham with its narrow-arched fifteenth-century bridge, beyond which one enters the wild and lovely marshland country surrounding Horsey

Mere, Hickling Broad(37) and Martham Broad. There one is in true Broadland country, unspoiled and much as it was two or three centuries ago. Hickling Broad, and its continuation, Heigham Sound, together cover something over 600 acres, a square mile of water. The surrounding reed-lands and marshes give an impression of even greater space. Seen at night or in the mists of winter, Hickling sometimes appears limitless.

Many large pike have been caught in Heigham Sound and the whole district is particularly notable for wildfowl, waders and rare birds. Bitterns are more or less an everyday sight, whilst the marsh harrier and Montagu's harrier both nest regularly on the Hickling and Horsey levels. The rare and beautiful little bearded tit, which at one time was almost extinct, and then like the bittern re-established itself, was more or less common on Hickling until the disastrously cold winter of 1947, when practically the entire breeding colony was wiped out. My friend, Mr. Roland Green, the eminent bird artist, who had his studio in the heart of a reed-bed on the shore of Hickling Broad, where he painted his enchanting pictures of wildfowl and marshland scenes, told me at the time that only one cock-bird survived on the whole broad. Luckily the stock has now increased, and with reasonable luck these endearing mice-like little birds, with their sweet bell notes, should soon be reasonably common again.

There is an excellent old inn, "The Pleasure Boat", at the far end of Hickling Broad, but apart from a few picturesque cottages, one or two drainage mills and the thatched roof of Whiteslea Lodge, once the home of the late Lord Desborough, not another house is visible from the broad itself.

The visitor to Hickling will never find it unduly crowded in summer, for the simple reason that most of the broad is so shallow that motor-cruisers and the larger yachts find it quite impossible to leave the deep-water channel across the middle of the broad which, like that on Breydon Water, is marked by guide-posts.

In winter the broad is populated by thousands of coots and some-times thousands of wild duck as well as geese and wild swans. The annual Hickling coot shoot is an exhilarating affair in which thirty to forty punts take part. The coots are driven by the line of boats from one end of the broad to the other until they take wing and come rocketing back over the boats, travelling high and fast. I have taken part in a coot shoot when over 600 have been shot in a day, but that total has been almost doubled on one or two other occasions.

The broad is surrounded by thousands of acres of quaking reed-beds, hidden "pulk holes", sedge fens and half-drained grazing marshes, the haunt of otters, bitterns, harriers, short-eared owls and every sort of wildfowl.

From Heigham Sound, where in January 1949, a 35½-pound pike was caught by a man who had never caught a pike before in his life, the Meadow Dyke leads through a wilderness of sedge, reeds and sallow bushes to Horsey Mere, an enchanting little lake of about 100 acres, almost circular, with an island in the middle. It lies within sight and smell of the sea, which is less than a mile distant. Horsey is lonely and lovely, without a house on its banks, almost entirely surrounded by marshes and reed-beds and, on a day of bright sun, as blue as the Mediterranean.

At the north-west corner of the mere lies the great reed-bed known as Braydon Marsh, more than 100 acres of jungle, stronghold of otters.

The mere and the marsh form part of the Horsey Hall estate of some 1,600 acres which Major Anthony Buxton has devised to the National Trust. He continues to live at the hall which, in the last century, was the home of that wonderful shot and good naturalist, the late Captain Robert Rising, whose collection of Norfolk birds was almost unique.

Horsey is a charming little village with a reed-thatched church, a few scattered flint-built cottages, an inn called "The Nelson Head", and a village shop which sells everything. Crees, Major Buxton's gamekeeper, who lives in a thatched cottage on the roadside, is a good naturalist and a most interesting man. He knows the habits and movements of every poacher within miles and is a fount of knowledge on rare birds. Among the rarities recorded from Horsey are the osprey, the purple gallinule, black terns, which are regular visitors, garganey, gadwall and the harriers and bitterns which are regular inhabitants. Less than two years ago I saw no less than seven bitterns in a week and three harriers in a day on the Martham and Horsey marshes.

A biggish dyke known as The Cut leads from the Braydon end

of Horsey Mere through the flat, reclaimed marshes of the Brograve Level, on which I had the shooting for some seasons, to the lonely church and gauntly beautiful hall at Waxham. Waxham Hall was built about the middle of the fifteenth century, of faced flints with stone quoins. It is neither large nor small, but a village manor-house of the middle sort. It is surrounded on the sea side by a tall embattled wall with a square, pinnacled gateway. It lies right under great sandhills which, in places, rise to 100 feet or so. Stand on those hills, with the empty vastness of the North Sea on one hand, the green marshes and shining waterways on the other side and the bleakly lovely church standing almost in the farmyard at one's feet, and one gets a true sense of the austere beauty of this lonely land.

Martham Broad, which lies farther up the Thurne, and is the remotest of all the broads, can only be reached by returning through Heigham Sound and Kendal Dyke to the main river. The broad is divided in two by dense reed-beds, is privately owned and almost unnavigable, except in a punt, owing to the dense growth of weeds which choke its waters in summer. For some years I had the shooting on both broads, which formed part of the Burnley Hall estate of some 1,500 acres—a wild and beautiful place, where one could see harriers and bitterns daily and shoot anything from snipe and woodcock to pheasants and wild geese. Burnley Hall is a medium-sized, red-brick Georgian house, once the seat of Joseph Hume, M.P., the champion of freedom, and, later, the home of my old friend, the late Sir Gerald Talbot. It now belongs to Major Kenneth Watt.

West Somerton village, which lies at the head of the dyke beyond Martham Broad, is a pleasant, lost and forgotten little place of thatched cottages, with an inn at the crossroads, a ruined church in the hall grounds and ancient memories of bloody battles with the Danes. A mile beyond it, hidden in the sandhills, lies the bleak little fishing village of Winterton, with a magnificent church and the claim to be perhaps the most easterly village in all England. Defoe wrote that he found this village half built from the timbers of wrecked ships. Within the last eighty years the Winterton lifeboat has saved more than 500 lives.

Winterton and the equally bleak and lonely villages of Sea

Palling, Happisburgh and Bacton, which lie scattered along this almost uninhabited coast to the north, have a character of their own, an atmosphere blent of great and lonely spaces of land and sea.

The broads which lie to the south and west of the Hickling area can only be reached by sailing back down the Thurne until the Bure is reached at Thurne Mouth. There the river winds through flat marshes past the few grey and sere ruins of St. Benet's Abbey (41), the noble and pathetic remnants of a once great house. A solitary arch and a few fragments of flint walls are all that mark the burial ground of that challenging figure of the Middle Ages, Sir John Fastolf, Governor of the Bastille, Seneschal, Lieutenant, and Regent of Normandy, and Governor of Anjou and Maine. To-day the rabbits burrow amid the forgotten bones of the hero of Agincourt and the wild geese clang their lonely requiem for the great dead beneath the bitter winter stars.

Throughout the Middle Ages the Abbey of St. Benet-at-Holm was great and powerful. Its walls and buildings covered some 38 acres of ground. About it were the waters and the marshes. The abbey possessed vast lands and many manors. It was not suppressed, as were so many others, in 1537, but later the buildings fell into decay and practically the whole place was pulled down and its stones taken by barge to Norwich to build the now-vanished Duke's Palace of the Dukes of Norfolk.

William the Conqueror besieged St. Benet's Abbey with a fleet of boats and a small army of men, but the monks held out against him until the Normans took prisoner one of their number, named Ethelwald, who turned traitor. As I have written elsewhere in *Marshland Adventure*:

Ethelwald returned to the Abbey and, on the appointed night, threw open the great gate. The Norman soldiers surged in, and, amid the flare of torches, the wild clanging of bells, the whistling of arrows, clash of swords, and screams of the wounded and dying, the Abbey was taken and the defenders slain.

Then Ethelwald was led by sardonic Norman knights to the High Altar in the great Abbey church, dim-lit by swealing candles and smoking torches, and there, dressed in the Abbot's robe, the mitre was placed on his head and he was installed as Abbot of the monastery while, without, the dying monks lay writhing in their blood, and the Fenmen who had aided their defence kicked in halters from the battlements.

Then, on that night of high and bloody tragedy, the Normans led the new Abbot, proud in his Judas pride, to the topmost tower of the high church. They snatched the mitre from his head. They stripped the cope from his shoulders. They put a halter about his neck. And the pale traitor, screaming in his base agony, was thrown from the tower to dangle kicking at the end of the rope. That is the tale.

And they say that if you go ashore on Cowholm Marshes, alone, on a cold night of moon, you will see a black figure, choking and kicking at a rope's end from the high arch that still stands—the traitor, his robes flapping in death like a black crow in a snare.

A little below St. Benet's Abbey and Thurne mouth a narrow dyke leads up to the remote village of Upton, with its land-locked broad, privately owned, and the haunt of bitterns, otters, wild duck and great pike. There are one or two rowing-boats on the broad, which is almost entirely surrounded by swampy woods and forests of reeds. The broad is deep in parts and the mud is even deeper than the water. It would never surprise me if someone were to take a pike of 30 pounds or more from this forgotten pool.

Upton Hall, a square brick building near the church, was for many years the home of the Broom family, who owned and farmed some 2,000 acres in the district. That good old sportsman, foxhunter and yachtsman, Mr. H. S. Broom, spent his childhood there and, on the collapse of the family fortune, went from this lonely Broadland home to earn his living as a mechanic and, by dint of hard work and skill, built up the great engineering firm of Broom-Wade Ltd. which to-day is world-famous.

Almost opposite St. Benet's Abbey another dyke leads through marshes yellow with kingcups and flagged with irises to South Walsham Broad, a charming little lake in a woodland setting with a red-brick Elizabethan hall, standing blandly in its little park above the waters. South Walsham is one of the prettier and less-frequented broads and forms part of the South Walsham Hall estate of some 800 acres, which formerly belonged to that splendid old sportsman, Sir Bartle Frere. It is now owned by Major the Hon. Henry Broughton.

Less than half a mile by road from South Walsham Broad lies the enchanting village and broad of Ranworth with the wild Ranworth Fens bordering the main river for some miles. Ranworth Broad (36) can only be reached by way of Ranworth Dyke, which leads first to the sweetly pretty little Maltsters' Broad, with an inn, a green and grassy landing-stage, a boat dock and a colony of "wild" ducks so tame that they eat out of one's hand. Ranworth Broad itself, which covers rather more than 100 acres, can only be visited by permission of the owner, Lt.-Col. Henry Cator of Woodbastwick Hall, an estate of some 7,000 acres which shows some of the best wildfowl and pheasant shooting in the country. The late King George VI frequently shot on the Ranworth Fens where, if they chose to go out for record bags, wildfowl could be shot in hundreds. Colonel Cator, however, is no believer in excessive shooting for shooting's sake. Thanks to his policy of strict preservation, Ranworth Broad is an absolute sanctuary of duck and, to a large extent, supplies the surrounding marshes with their stocks of resident wildfowl.

A year or so ago, Colonel Cator decided to throw Ranworth Broad open to the public, but this public-spirited gesture was almost immediately ruined by hooligan "bird-lovers", who proceeded to pillage every available nest on the broad. The not unnatural result is that the visitor to Ranworth to-day must first apply to the gamekeeper for permission to enter its waters so far as the western part is concerned.

Ranworth Church is quite the loveliest in the whole of Broadland. It possesses a unique treasure in the shape of the famous Ranworth Missal or Sarum Antiphoner, a superbly illuminated book of early medieval workmanship. I doubt if it is surpassed by any similar work in England other than the Luttrell Psalter. The church contains a painted screen (40) of incredible beauty, which has been described as "suggestive of a great initial page of some splendidly illuminated manuscript". The paintings are said to have been the work of German members of the School of Meister Wilhelm of Cologne, who settled in Norwich during the fifteenth century at a time when this church was building.

Ranworth Church has been well restored within recent years. It owes much of its stately beauty to the generosity of Flemish weavers who had a colony in the village more than 400 years ago. There is an attractive Elizabethan manor-house in the village, many charming

40 Ranworth Church, Norfolk: a panel of the late fifteenth-century painted
Screen depicting St. Michael

41 St. Benet's Abbey, in the Cowholm Marshes, Norfolk. The fifteenth-
century Gatehouse surrounds a drainage mill

42 Looking across Breydon Water, Norfolk, towards Great Yarmouth

old cottages and a parson who is justly proud of his lovely church and its Missal. The Missal, incidentally, was written by the monks of Langley Abbey and consists of 285 pages of sheepskin illustrated by twenty brilliant pictures coloured with vegetable dyes and gold leaf. It was stolen in the reign of Henry VI and was lost until about 1850, when a collector bought it for fifty guineas. At his death it came into the possession of a Bond Street bookseller, who asked the vicar £500 for it. The sum was raised within eighteen months. The Missal and the painted screen between them attract as many as 20,000 people in a year to the church.

There are many charming walks in the neighbourhood and two small broads, Cockshoot Broad and Decoy Broad, both of about 10 acres in extent and both private and strictly preserved. If such broads were not kept private, there is not the slightest doubt that the remainder of Broadland would lose much of its unique bird life. Such broads act as reservoirs of wildfowl where they may nest and breed in safety.

Ranworth is a village of ghosts. First there is the dramatic spectre of Colonel the Hon. Thomas Sidney, who, on December 31st, 1770, is said to have been kidnapped by the Devil, who threw him over the pommel of his saddle on a seventeen-hand ghostly hunter and then galloped madly across the broad, each hoof-mark on the water raising a jet of steam! This ghastly steeplechase takes place each year at midnight on the last day of the year, for those who have eyes to see.

Then there is the "whistling" ghost, in a certain house which shall be nameless, but which my friend, Mr. Alan Savory, declares he has heard. I prefer the third of the Ranworth ghosts, that of the gentle monk Pacificus, who redecorated the Ranworth rood-screen in 1538. On summer evenings the brown-habited wraith of the old monk is said to row up Ranworth Dyke in a ghostly boat of antique design with the friendly spectre of his little dog sitting beside him.

Two miles up-river from Ranworth Dyke lies the charming little village of Horning, just past Horning Ferry, whose beautiful old inn, "The Ferry", was unfortunately almost entirely destroyed by a bomb during the war. Horning is a bright and gaily delightful village of picturesque cottages, comfortable inns, busy boat-yards, a place of white sails in summer and grimly freezing pike-fishermen in winter. The Swan Hotel contains a magnificently terrifying array of monster pike, unbelievable perch and other startling fish from local waters. Horning, in fine, is an excellent place from which to start a cruise through the chain of broads which connect with the main river.

Above Horning the river banks become more wooded, one sees more pheasants than wild duck, and sailing is sometimes a problem because the dense belts of woodland along the river blanket the breeze. A little way beyond the village lies Hoveton Little Broad, privately owned by Captain T. C. R. Blofield, the head of one of the oldest families in Norfolk. He also owns the adjoining Hoveton Great Broad and allows public access to part of his waters. Hoveton has a wonderful gullery, where black-headed gulls breed each year in hundreds. Some large pike have been taken out of the broad and more than once over 100 pounds weight of fish has been caught in a day. The Great Broad usually produces one or two 20-pounders each season.

Opposite Hoveton Great Broad lies the charming little Salhouse Broad, one of the prettiest small broads on the river. It is full of good rudd which will sometimes take a fly. Green and park-like meadows rise in a gentle slope from one end of the broad, whilst the other end is heavily wooded, altogether forming a charming picture of wood-land, meadow and water. Salhouse Hall, which lies in a park near the church, is a good old Elizabethan house with a fifteenth-century door, and is the home of a family who have been squires of the parish for many generations. The church tower is said to be 600 years old, the font is medieval and the two coffin stones under the tower are 700 years old. There is some good glass in one window, showing the Women at the Tomb, which came from Bruges. Altogether, Salhouse has everything to commend it which age and beauty can confer.

A mile up-stream lies Wroxham Broad, large and lovely and much too popular in summer. It is an ideal broad for sailing, with a well-run Yacht Club, first-class fishing and charming countryside surroundings. The result is, of course, that far too many people go there. Personally, I prefer Wroxham or, indeed, any other broad in autumn after the first sharp frosts have sent the majority of the "water-hikers" home and have turned the reed-beds and marshland levels into seas of glowing colour, orange and rusty red, yellow and gold. Sometimes in winter one has seen hundreds of wild duck rise from the empty waters of Wroxham where, on a busy week-end in summer, a moorhen dare hardly show its beak. Wroxham village, which nowadays is almost a small town, is full of boat-builders, of whom my genial friend, Jack Powles, is king, with several good inns and a vast emporium run by the ingenious Mr. Roy, which advertises itself, no doubt with complete truth, as "The Largest Village Store in England". You can buy everything there from children's clothing and cigars to fishing rods, butcher's meat and plate powder.

Above Wroxham Bridge the river enters a wooded country of steep little valleys and green little hills which someone once christened "Little Switzerland". The river winds and twists around the foot of the hill on which stands Belaugh Church, past the woods and park of Wroxham Hall, the seat of Major S. W. Trafford, who owns about 6,000 acres, and so, twisting and turning, pursues its inconsequent course to the picture-postcard village of Coltishall, where the great white-gabled bulk of Horstead Mill(35) straddles the river. You cannot go any farther. A lock sees to that. It is probably one of the most painted mills in all England, and has appeared in the Royal Academy at least a score of times. Coltishall is a charming village built on a low hill with riverside gardens that are a delight to the eye.

Chapter
VII

THE ENCHANTING WATERS
OF THE ANT

VII

HALF the charm of Broadland waters is their diversity. No two rivers are quite alike and no two broads are exactly similar. True, the Thurne, flowing through flat marshland country, is much like the lower reaches of the Bure, but quite different from the upper waters of that stream when it tries to lose itself amid the miniature green precipices of "Little Switzerland" and finally vanishes into the unguessed pastoral hinterland that lies behind Horstead Mill. There, beyond the pleasant meads of Buxton Lammas, you enter a land asleep with memories of the Middle Ages, for the Pastons lived in their great hall at Oxnead, of which there is still a stately fragment, whilst Ann Boleyn dwelt at Blickling(43), that most perfectly proportioned Tudor house. That, after all, is out of the Broadland country and no place for a man in a boat unless it be of the smallest size and most shallow draught.

If, however, you sail up that narrow and serpentine little river called the Ant(56), which joins the Bure just below Horning Hall and just above St. Benet's Abbey, you enter waters that are unique and comparatively little known. For the first half-mile or so of its course, the Ant flows, or rather twists and winds, through flat cattle marshes where, in winter, you may see wild geese and in summer you are more than likely to encounter a sharp-tempered Friesian bull. These are the marshes belonging to Ludham Hall, farmed for many years by that great character and shrewd farmer, Mr. William Wright. Ludham Old Hall was originally a seat of the powerful Abbots of St. Benet's Abbey. Then it became a country-house of the Bishops of Norwich. Most of the early house, which was good and spacious, was burnt down in 1611, but the original old brick chapel, built by Bishop Harsnet, still stands and is used as a barn. It is worth a passing examination, for it lies no more than a short walk from Ludham Bridge, which here spans the Ant. The bridge is flanked by one of those useful Broadland village stores where you can buy anything that man, woman or boat is likely to require (44, 45).

Beyond the bridge one enters a wilder area of marshes and reed-beds with dense carrs of willow dotted here and there and, commanding the whole, a biggish, pleasant-looking house with a thatched roof crowning How Hill, that surprising little eminence which bobs up like a green Gibraltar above the marshes on the right-hand side of the river. At the back of How Hill lies a small private water known as Crome's Broad which, on occasion, is packed with wild duck. There is another small broad hidden half a mile away to the left, known as Alderfen Broad, but I have never been there and I am told that it is almost entirely grown up. It can be reached if you go by way of the hamlet of Irstead Street.

Irstead itself, small and charming and bowered in trees, with a good church where William of Wykeham was vicar, lies on the river bank a little farther on, a forgotten place with a nice little Elizabethan hall which fits with singular grace into its surroundings of rolling fields, massed woods and swampy valleys.

Just beyond Irstead the scene changes. The wild waste of Barton Broad opens up, a gleaming sheet of water, fringed by acres of waving reeds, dotted with reedy islands and seeming to stretch into infinity. It is actually rather more than a mile long and, next to Hickling, the largest broad in Norfolk. It has the same quality of wildness that belongs to Hickling and is surrounded by swamps as dense and dangerous as any which fringe the low shores of Hickling. Away to the right, as one enters the broad, lies the incredible wilderness of the Catfield Fens, a place of hidden pulk-holes, black bottomless mud, narrow reedy channels and jungles of sedge, in which a stranger could lose himself and drown with comparative ease. For many years Catfield Hall was the home of that good naturalist and wonderful shot, Lord William Percy, who in these fens carried out his remarkable series of investigations into the habits of the bittern and the use of the "powder puff" which the bird conceals beneath its feathers and uses in order to rid itself of the slime with which it covers its feathers after a busy morning catching eels.

43　Blickling Hall, Norfolk (1626): the South Front

44   The Church: fifteenth-century with a late fourteenth-century chancel

45   Thatched cottages in the village street

LUDHAM VILLAGE

Lord William is not one of those eager "bird-watchers" who dash into print, burst upon the air and smirk at us from the television screen on every possible occasion in order to impress upon the world that they, and they alone, are experts. Yet I doubt if any man alive knows more about wildfowl and their habits than this tall, sinewy, retiring son of the House of Percy who has been to practically every wild corner of the earth in order to watch and study rare birds. The series of photographs of bitterns which he took in the Catfield Fens is unique and constitutes a most valuable addition to our knowledge of the habits of that notably retiring bird.

Barton Broad is, luckily, never overcrowded with craft. That is partly because of the narrow sinuousness of its parent river, the Ant, partly because nothing drawing much more than 3 feet can safely navigate the river and, also, because the broad itself is full of shallows, floating "hovers" and anchored "bolders". Indeed, it has shown an alarming tendency to grow up and shrink in size during the last two years, the inevitable result of which would be to rob the public of free waters and add free acres to the territories of riparian owners. However, that danger seems likely to be averted by public action and before long we may find that many of the grown-up waters surrounding Barton Broad may be dredged out and reopened. This is particularly needed at Sutton Broad at the northern end of Barton, which was once a broad of nearly 100 acres of water and is now merely a narrow channel running through impassable reed-beds.

Barton is a home of great pike. Many have been taken there between 20 and 30 pounds in weight, and there are plenty of big ones still waiting to be caught. An arm of the broad, which runs past a belt of tall woodlands immediately to the left, as one enters the broad, leads to the fascinating little Gay's Staithe—no more than a farmhouse, a few cottages, a green landing-stage and a roadside inn, at the head of a woodland waterway, which might well be anywhere except on the Norfolk Broads. Yet, within half a mile, one is back in a flat, wild reedy wilderness of an entirely different character. Such is the diversity of Barton.

At the far end of the broad lies the little hamlet of Barton Staithe, where is an ancient yellow-fronted off-licence, sitting under two oak trees, which will sell you beer out of the back window in its back-yard. The men of Barton Staithe and the near-by village of Barton Turf are all boat-builders, wherry owners, wildfowlers, fishermen and broadsmen. The Hewitts, the Hayletts and the Coxes have been sailing these waters and catching their fish for the last four or five centuries. The great-grandfather of my old friend, William Hewitt, one Robert Hewitt, who died at the age of sixty in 1838, was the man who, it is claimed, taught Nelson to sail a boat. That was when young Nelson was a schoolboy, twelve years of age, at the Paston Grammar School at North Walsham. Nelson's sister rented Barton Broad in those days from a Mr. Morse and the Admiral-to-be used to come down and stay with her at the hall.

The last punt-gunner to shoot for a living on Barton Broad was old "Pinny" Cox, who used a muzzle-loading swivel-gun, firing half a pound of shot, up to about sixty years ago. At that time there were five or six punters on the broad and it was not uncommon for any one of them to kill thirty or forty ducks in the morning. Nowadays no punt-guns are used on any broads except on Breydon Water which, when one considers their comparatively limited size, is perhaps just as well. A good punt-gun will throw its charge of shot 150 yards.

At the Gay's Staithe end of the broad lies the park and ancient hall of Beeston where the Preston family have dwelt for many centuries. Jacob Preston was one of the few faithful Royalist gentlemen who attended Charles I on the scaffold. The ring which the king gave him a few moments before the axe fell is still preserved at the hall.

Beeston is a good sporting estate and the present owner, Sir Edward Preston, Bart., is an energetic, practical farmer who runs his 4,000-acre property in a business-like way, with close personal attention to every detail. He knows every man, boy and woman on the place by name, and when the cost of living went up he lowered the rents of his cottage pensioners in order to make life easier for them.

I have happy memories of Barton. I think of wild, winter days, of tossing reeds and white waves, of grey clouds scudding before the North Sea gale and the brave sight of a score of grey geese coming in high over the Catfield Fens and landing in a reedy bay in a sheet of foam. There were pochards shooting like bullets over the running waves and mallard in teams etched against the sky—and not a boat in sight, not a man nor sail, to spoil the wild beauty of it all.

I think of bright days of early spring, fishing for pike at the tail-end of the season on a sharp, blue morning and hooking a 12-pounder off the reed-bed where lie the bold hulls of two gallant old wherries, *Victory of Barton* and *Wanderer;* old *Wanderer,* who was a queen upon the shining rivers of Suffolk and Norfolk when Victoria was young upon her throne.

There are memories of shooting partridges and hares and great brilliant marsh-bred pheasants on the Catfield farmlands, where reed-beds merge into swampy meadows full of snipe and you come to the first firm ground strong enough to take the plough.

There was a golden afternoon in a gun-punt, sailing, silent as a ghost, up that waterway which they call Padder's Lane, through the rustling reedy wilderness of Sutton Broad, up Sutton Dyke beyond to Sutton Staithe, where there is a pleasant old red-brick inn, now a club, full of good bits of old furniture, bright brass, shining copper and such harmless antiquities.

On that quiet voyage through rustling reeds and white lilies I saw, sweeping low over the reed-tops, the sudden, blue-grey vision of a Montagu's harrier, and then, to cap it, flushed a bittern from the rond not 100 yards farther on. So few people sail on Barton or explore its waterways and bays, its reedy channels and quaking ronds, that you may expect to see anything there, from a bittern crouching in the reeds to a black tern glistening bluely in the sun, in slow and graceful flight.

There is another dyke which runs up to Stalham, but Stalham is a dull little town, prim, and only good for shopping. Beyond it, when Nelson was learning to sail on Barton, there lay another little broad at Dilham, but that to-day is a mere grown-up reed-fen. Beyond that, the upper reaches of the Ant pursue a still-sinuous course through wooded and agricultural scenery, past Honing with its locks and mills, skirting the market town of North Walsham until, finally, the stream loses itself in Antingham Ponds, which are too remote, too small and too shallow for anyone but a born Red Indian to attempt to reach.

For my part I could be happy amid the reedy wastes of Barton, the bays of Hickling or upon the bosom of Horsey Mere without any wish to travel farther afield. For in such wild places is all richness of beauty.

46 Acle Church

Chapter
VIII

BIRDS, BEASTS AND FISHES
OF THE BROADS

A Paradise of Wildfowl

Bitterns and Harriers

Some Rare Waders

Uncommon Gulls

"Reed-Pheasants"

Otters and Nutria

The Best Coarse Fishing in England

VIII

NO part of England is richer in bird life, particularly un-common species, or in the size and quantity of coarse fish, than the district known as Broadland. If we were to draw a line from Sea Palling to North Walsham and thence to Aylsham and Norwich, south to Bungay and then east to Pakefield near Lowestoft, we should enclose an area which can show almost every bird, animal and fish on the British list. Even trout can be included, whilst salmon are not uncommonly netted off the coast. The reason for the extraordinary richness and diversity of bird life lies in the fact that the blunt north-east shoulder of Norfolk, the most easterly part of England jutting boldly into the North Sea, is the first land which migratory birds from the Baltic countries, Holland, Germany and Belgium, sight on their autumn flights across the North Sea.

The deep woodlands, wide marshes and glittering waters of the Broads offer them immediate sanctuary, food and rest. The result is a unique annual spring and autumn migration, coupled with a large and extraordinarily varied breeding population.

Many of the rarest birds on the British list, including certain unique species which have occurred once or twice only, have been recorded from the district. That is due not only to the accident of geography which makes the area the first landing-ground for overseas migrants, but also to the fact that it is a natural resting-place for many birds which pursue a north-to-south or south-to-north migration along the east coast of England. For example, immature golden eagles not infrequently journey from Scotland to the Pyrenees, whilst peregrines and other birds of prey follow the same route. In addition to the natural attractions offered by the Broads, there are in the area a number of sanctuaries, many of them privately owned small broads, which give complete security to visiting birds and those which are resident. Indeed, the natural history of Broadland owes an imperishable debt to the many public-spirited land-owners and great naturalists who, for a century or more, have given sanctuary to its bird life and have studied its birds, animals and fishes with intelligence and meticulous accuracy.

Just as Norwich produced its individual School of Painters, so Norfolk, and more particularly the Broadland, has produced its own school of naturalists, of whom Sir Thomas Browne was perhaps the first, and its own peculiarly rich range of literature dealing with its wild life.

Among the earliest writers were Sir James Paget and his brother C. J. Paget who, in 1834, produced that very readable and reliable little book, *A Sketch of the Natural History of Yarmouth and Its Neighbourhood*, which gives a remarkable picture of wild life on Breydon a century and a quarter ago, with many anecdotes of the unlettered and uncouth brotherhood of wildfowlers and fishermen who with punt-gun, shoulder-gun, net and eel spear lived a primitive existence on that waste of water and earned a precarious living by bitter toil and hardy adventure.

Later came the Rev. Richard Lubbock with his carefully documented and charmingly written *Observations on the Fauna of Norfolk*, the third volume of which was completed by another great naturalist, Thomas Southwell, F.Z.S. Another parson, the Rev. Churchill Babington, produced *A Catalogue of the Birds of Suffolk*, which includes many references to the Broads. Then, over a period of years, my old friend, the late Arthur Patterson, produced a series of books dealing exclusively with Broads wild life which, in their own sphere, are unique. No lover of the Broads should be without Patterson's *Notes of an East Coast Naturalist*, *Wild Life on a Norfolk Estuary*, *A Norfolk Naturalist*, *Man and Nature on Tidal Waters* or *Wildfowlers and Poachers*, written shortly before he died. His little monograph, *A Catalogue of the Birds of Great Yarmouth*, republished in 1901, of which he gave me one of the only two copies partly bound in red leather, is rare but good. Patterson was a remarkable man. Born of humble parents, he began life running barefooted on the fish quays of Yarmouth, was more or less self-taught, became an attendant at a penny zoo, was the friend and confidant of every fisherman and wildfowler for miles around and, finally attaining

47 The evening flight on a Norfolk Broad

48 Spoonbills — rare but occasional visitors to Breydon. They once nested at Reedham

49 Bittern and young— now comparatively common on the remoter broads

NORFOLK WILDFOWL

some little financial security as a school attendance officer, he poured out book after book, article after article, all packed with rich and racy descriptions of primitive Broadland characters, together with extraordinarily detailed and accurate observations and records of bird, fish and animal life.

I am glad to say that before his death he not only received scientific honours, but was presented by the Lord Lieutenant of his county with a purse of gold and an illuminated address in recognition of his work for the natural history of Broadland.

In more recent years Dr. B. B. Riviere has produced an exhaustive and up-to-date *History of the Birds of Norfolk* which, if read in conjunction with Mr. Claud B. Ticehurst's *History of the Birds of Suffolk*, will give one a good overall picture of the present-day bird life of this fascinating region. I would suggest adding to it the scarce little *Notes on the Birds of Cley, Norfolk,* by the late H. N. Pashley, published in 1925. Cley is outside the Broads area, being some miles to the north, but the records collected by Pashley who, like Patterson, was the village naturalist and an accomplished taxidermist, are mainly of birds which belong naturally to the Broadland area.

Finally, there are the excellent chapters on bird life, fish life, entomology and botany in Dutt's charming book, *The Norfolk Broads*, published in 1903, and most beautifully illustrated in colour by the late Frank Southgate, one of the best marshland artists of bird life that England ever knew. His tradition is carried on to-day by Mr. Roland Green, the bird artist of Hickling.

When we come to consider the present-day wild life of Broadland, the outstanding fact which must gratify every naturalist is that certain species, once extinct or nearly so, have now returned to breed and are becoming comparatively common again.

The notable examples are the bittern (49) and the bearded tit, that enchanting little reed bunting with the delicately pencilled moustaches and fascinating bell-like notes which the marshmen call "reed-pheasants". Before long it is not too much to hope that the avocet, the black tern, the ruff and reeve and the spoonbill (48) may all re-establish themselves as breeding residents in the countryside which was once their stronghold. Avocets have already returned to breed within the last few years on certain remote marshes in Suffolk, where they are strictly protected, and there is every reason to hope that these colonies may extend their range to the Broads.

Wildfowl are, naturally, the largest and most interesting section of Broadland birds. First and noblest are the wild swans. Both whoopers and Bewick swans turn up each winter, more or less frequently, particularly on Hickling Broad, Horsey Mere and Breydon Water and occasionally on Barton Broad. I have seen as many as thirty wild swans rise in a sheet of foam and a windy music of wings from the great reedy bay of Swim Coots on Hickling Broad on a day of steely, winter sky when between 400 and 500 mallard(51), widgeon, pochard and teal were crossing and re-crossing the wild sweep of sky in never-ending skeins and teams— a picture of unforgettable majesty, reminiscent of a steel engraving from Folkard's ancient classic, *The Wildfowler*. The Polish swan is said to have occurred on a number of occasions, but these should be treated with reserve. Riviere certainly does not include it in his list.

Many mute swans breed on all the broads in considerable numbers. In my view there are too many of them. These birds, lovely to look at, are the most unmitigated tyrants, bullies and prigs and inevitably drive wild duck away from any stretch of water which they regard as their kingdom. It is an undoubted fact that they will seize young ducklings, hold them under water and drown them. For this reason, when I had the shooting on Martham Broad, I religiously shot every mute swan which attempted to take up its residence. The result was that we had plenty of duck nesting in peace and security and roast swan, a by no means despicable dish, for the flesh is close, darkish and a little sweet, almost like venison, was frequently on my table and those of many of the villagers.

It is quite possible that the whooper swan, that magnificent wild trumpeter of the winter skies, who should never be shot under any circumstances, may return one day to breed. Early in the spring of 1928, a friend, the present Lord Walsingham, who owns the Merton estate of some 12,000 acres in South-west Norfolk, which includes two large meres, Stanford Water and Tomston Mere, and a number of smaller meres, wrote to tell me that a pair of whooper swans had started to build a nest at the foot of a willow tree on a tiny island in Westmere. One of the birds had an injured leg, which probably accounted for the pair of them remaining behind in England. They were strong on the wing and built a nest of dead rushes and water-weeds which, however, was deserted by May 12th. Those two erudite Norfolk naturalists, Dr. Sydney Long of the Norfolk and Norwich Naturalists' Trust, and Mr. Hugh Wormald, both saw these swans and identified them as genuine whoopers.

Wild swans nested in Norfolk and in the fens of Cambridgeshire and Lincolnshire in the past. With protection and security from the prying attentions of so-called "bird-watchers", whose camera-snooping activities frighten far too many birds from the nest in the spring, with the result that the eggs become unfertile, there is just a possibility that one day they may return to breed.

Almost every wild goose on the British list visits the Broads. The commoner varieties are the greylag and pinkfoot. The latter can be seen in thousands each winter on certain marshes. The white-fronted goose is not quite so common, whilst the brent turns up in varying numbers, according to the severity of the weather, on Breydon. The bernacle is an irregular winter visitor. The Canada goose, originally introduced as an ornament on the big lakes in Gunton Park and Holkham Park in North Norfolk, has now become comparatively common and is gradually extending its range throughout the Broads. Several examples of the Egyptian goose, one of which is in my collection, have occurred from time to time, but these were almost certainly escapes from private waters.

Snow geese have been recorded from Cley and Holkham in North Norfolk, but I have no record of them in the Broads area. On the other hand, a specimen of the extremely rare red-breasted goose is said to have been shot on the Halvergate marshes in 1805. It was bought in Yarmouth market by an odd little bird-dealer named Lilly Wigg, one of a race of self-taught naturalists who earned a precarious living in the last century by selling rare specimens to wealthy collectors. He, little realising what a rarity was in his hands, plucked it and ate it. It was afterwards identified by the feathers, to the eternal regret of the lamenting Mr. Wigg, who could easily have obtained £10 or £20 for his specimen.

Among the duck which frequent the Broads, the commonest is the mallard (51), which, with the teal, breeds in large quantities. Widgeon, locally called "smee", are common in winter and are frequently on Breydon in thousands. Pochard, tufted duck, scaup, shoveller, and golden-eye are all fairly common. Pintail are not uncommon in winter and are frequently taken in the decoy at Fritton Lake, where I saw four or five specimens of this singularly graceful and handsome duck on my last visit, sitting comfortably in a wire cage, waiting to be sent to a life of fatted ease on the lake in St. James's Park.

Among the real rarities which have occurred from time to time are the ruddy shell-duck, four of which were seen by A. Nudd at Hickling in October 1916 and another at Breydon in 1918; the red-crested pochard, the first British example of which was shot on Breydon in 1818, since when a few others have been recorded from the district; the white-eyed pochard, which has occurred several times; the harlequin duck, said to have been killed near Yarmouth; the buffel-headed duck or morillon, the first of the only three British species of which was shot near Yarmouth about 1830; Steller's eider, the first of the only two British specimens of which was killed at Caister on February 10th, 1830; the very rare surf-scoter, three of which were identified by Miss Judith Ferrier, on November 16th, 1927, off Hemsby beach; the equally rare American hooded mer-ganser, one of which was obtained near Yarmouth in 1829; whilst the gadwall and graceful little garganey teal, distinctly uncommon in other parts of England, are by no means uncommon on the Broads.

Sea-going ducks include that handsome fellow, the shell-duck, who can often be seen on Breydon, in dozens and scores. Scaup, although essentially a sea-duck, seem to visit Hickling Broad fairly regularly, but they are uncommon on the other broads. The graceful long-tailed duck, which I have shot off Holy Island, miles out at sea, arrives off the Norfolk coast in November and is seldom seen on the Broads, although one or two have been killed on Rockland. Another was shot on Hickling in 1856 and a third at Acle in 1885. The common eider occasionally turns up on Breydon, and one was found on Horsey Warren in 1918 after a gale. The common and velvet scoters are both frequently seen in winter, and the former occasionally

50   Redshank on the tide-edge on Breydon Water

51   Mallard on a broadland "Rond"

52 A Great-crested Grebe and its nest on Hickling Broad, Norfolk

53 A baby Otter in the Yare Valley

visits some of the broads. I shot one on Martham Broad in the winter of 1947. The red-breasted merganser and goosander are both winter visitors, and the latter occasionally turns up on Hickling and Fritton, as does the smew. They generally leave in March.

Cormorants are common on Breydon and, according to my friend Walter Mussett, the decoy-man at Fritton Lake, they still nest in a dead tree in the woods above the lake where, in 1825, there were regularly fifty or sixty nests each year. Cormorants may often be seen flying up the Bure or the Yare. The shag is relatively uncommon and usually in immature plumage. Gannets turn up off the coast in small numbers with the arrival of the herring shoals.

Sir Thomas Browne stated that he had in his collection "a pelican shott upon Horsey Fenne 1663 May 22", and he guessed at the time that it was "one of the King's pellicans lost at St. James's". Since then, no pelican had been seen in Norfolk until July 21st, 1926, when one flew in from the sea and alighted on Breydon. There it spent the night and, according to Dr. Riviere, left again the next morning at 9.30 a.m., in an easterly direction. A second pelican was recorded on Breydon on September 24th, 1915, and, when disturbed, "flew away to the north-east" and was never heard of again. It is a fascinating thought that both these birds may have been genuine wild specimens and not merely escapes.

The engaging little storm petrel turns up at sea most winters, sometimes in fair numbers. The much rarer Leach's fork-tailed petrel has been recorded forty or fifty times, one of the specimens being in my collection. Two extremely rare shearwaters, the Western Mediterranean and Madeiran varieties, have both been recorded from East Norfolk, one of the latter being picked up dead by a gamekeeper on the Earsham Hall estate on the Waveney in 1858. The Manx's shearwater is an occasional autumn visitor, whilst the great shearwater has been recorded from Lowestoft, Gorleston beach and Caister beach. The fulmar petrel is fairly common on the herring-grounds in autumn and winter.

That handsome enemy of fish, the great-crested grebe (52), which, in the middle of last century, was on the verge of extinction, is now common enough on nearly all broads, particularly the Trinity Broads. The Slavonian, red-necked and black-necked grebes are all winter visitors in small numbers, as is the great northern diver and black-throated diver. The little grebe is common on all broads and the red-throated diver is not uncommon on the coast. I have seen it in Meadow Dyke and on Horsey Mere.

Pallas's sand-grouse occurred at various places during the extra-ordinary immigrations of these Asiatic birds which took place on various dates in the latter half of last century. Twenty were seen at Hickling in 1906 and ten at Somerton in the same year.

The stone curlew or Norfolk plover, common enough on the Breckland, has turned up once or twice near Norwich, notably at Honingham, Taverham and Drayton as recently as 1929. Several specimens of the rare pratincole have been recorded from Breydon and Yarmouth, where, incidentally, the first British specimen of the Caspian plover was shot in 1890. Oyster-catchers, dotterel and ordinary ringed plover are fairly common round about Breydon and elsewhere, whilst the very rare little ringed plover is said to have been picked up dead at Surlingham in 1938.

Kentish plover, golden plover and grey plover are all winter migrants in fair numbers, whilst the peewit or lapwing is still common throughout Broadland, although its numbers have notably decreased elsewhere in England. The graceful little turnstone, with its fascinating changes of plumage, is not uncommon on Breydon, and I have seen them by the score on the beach at Waxham, Horsey and Somerton.

The ruff, once common as a breeding species, still turns up in spring and autumn in the Hickling and Horsey area, and it is to be hoped that before long they may breed again. Some reeves' eggs, brought from Holland, were put into redshanks' nests at Hickling in 1925 and seven of them hatched off.

Curlew and redshank(50) are common everywhere, particularly on Breydon. The latter, ringing their million bells of song, are among the most fascinating springtime nesting birds on the marshes. Sanderling, knots, dunlin, curlew sandpiper, little stints and Temminck's occur more or less regularly on migration. Various rare specimens of sandpiper, including the buff-breasted, the broad-billed and the red-breasted, have all been recorded. The purple sandpiper is common in autumn, as is the wood sandpiper and green sandpiper. That charming bird, the spotted redshank, of which I have six specimens all in different plumage, has turned up on Breydon, Barton and elsewhere. The greenshank is a regular migrant and the grey and red-necked phalaropes both occur in small numbers in spring and autumn. The much rarer black-winged stilt was last seen at Hickling in 1939, whilst the avocet is what one might describe as a "not-uncommon-rarity" on Breydon and, occasionally, on the marshes of the Bure. Bar-tailed and black-tailed godwits turn up in spring and autumn, and it is to be hoped that the latter will return to breed again before long. Whimbrel are common double-passage migrants. The great snipe has occurred on various occasions, whilst the common and jack snipe are found on practically every fen.

A bird which once bred in large numbers at Upton Broad and is now only seen occasionally as a migrant is the beautiful black tern. I have spent enchanted hours lying in a punt hidden among the reeds on Martham Broad, watching their slow and lazy flight, their plumage gleaming blue-black in the sunlight. They are seldom seen before May and usually return in August and September.

Extraordinary "falls" of woodcock sometimes occur on the coast in autumn under the "Woodcock Moon". When I had the shooting on the Burnley Hall estate, it was nothing uncommon for us to see twenty or thirty or more in a day. No less than 105 were shot in one day at Swanton Novers in 1872.

Common and Sandwich terns are both reasonably common nowadays, the former having re-established themselves as a breeding colony at Blakeney Point. The rare white-winged black tern has turned up on a number of occasions at Breydon and Horsey Mere, whilst the even rarer whiskered tern has been twice recorded from Hickling, in 1847 and in 1906. The gull-billed tern, another rarity, has occurred several times on Breydon, where the Caspian tern was seen in 1910 and, again, at sea, off Yarmouth in 1918. The Arctic tern is a winter migrant. The last record I have was of one at Hickling in April 1936. The little tern, a regular summer visitor, breeds at Horsey, whilst the rare roseate tern is now becoming a more frequent visitor to the coast.

Black-headed gulls abound on all the broads, whilst herring

gulls, common gulls, black-backed and lesser black-backed, are all birds of Breydon and the surrounding broads and marshes. Various examples of rarer gulls, including the very rare Mediterranean black-headed gull, have been recorded from Breydon. The skuas are all occasional autumn and winter visitors to the coast, as are guillemots and razor-bills.

That remarkably interesting bird, the great bustard, as large almost as a turkey, which once bred on the heaths of the Breckland, has occasionally turned up in the Broads area. I believe the last recorded specimen was seen on Somerton Warren by my keeper, Pateman, in the autumn of 1945. He described it to me as "a great, big, brownish bird with whiskers on his face and long legs about a yard high, that kept on walkin' about on the marsh under the sand-hills and only flew a few yards when I put him up. He came in from sea one morning, hung about here for several days and then cleared off". I have no doubt whatever from Pateman's careful description of the bird that this was a great bustard, of which, incidentally, I have a native Norfolk specimen, given me by the late Lord Walsing-ham and a native Cambridgeshire specimen, given me by J. C. M. Nichols, in my collection. Both are over a hundred years old. There is a magnificent case of these birds in the Norwich Castle Museum, where most of the other rarities I have mentioned can also be seen.

The late Captain Robert Rising saw a great bustard fly across Horsey Mere on January 7th, 1867, whilst, more recently, a female was shot at Costessey, near Norwich, on February 2nd, 1894. A specimen of the Eastern little bustard was shot in the same district at Hellesdon in 1835 and another on the Acle marshes in 1916. The crane is believed to have nested in the Broads district two or three hundred years ago. Odd specimens have turned up at different times over the years.

Among the crakes, the very rare little crake, of which I possess two specimens, has been recorded about a dozen times in Norfolk, including specimens from Buckenham Ferry in August 1827; Neatishead, on Barton Broad, in 1828; near Yarmouth in 1833; Horsey in 1833; Heigham Sounds in 1847; Dilham Fen in 1852; Catfield, near Hickling, in 1855; the Bure Marshes in 1867; and

Hickling in 1880. This tiny and secretive little bird may easily have occurred on other occasions without being recorded. Baillon's crake, which Gurney describes as "very rare but less so than the Little Crake", has been recorded from Barton Fen, Dilham, Buckenham Fen, Potter Heigham and Sutton Broad, where a nest with one egg was found in 1889. I have two specimens which are supposed to have been killed in Norfolk. The spotted crake, also rare, of which I have three specimens, is known to have nested at Hickling, Brunstead and Potter Heigham. Within recent years a nest was discovered on the edge of Hickling Broad by my grand old friend, Henry Whittaker, who, at eighty-seven, bright-eyed and bearded like a bush, is a splendid specimen of the old type of broadsman.

Major Anthony Buxton, of Horsey Hall, tells me that Sir Samuel Hoare, now Lord Templewood, definitely identified the very rare purple gallinule at Horsey in, I think, the 1930s, whilst the green-backed gallinule has turned up at Martham, Horning, Barton Broad and Hickling. It is possible that many of the latter may have been escapes from the Duke of Bedford's remarkable zoo at Woburn Abbey, where no less than sixty were turned down in 1897. The latest occurrence, of which I have a record, was at Barton Broad on October 13th, 1913. An example of the very rare Allen's gallinule was caught alive on a fishing-boat off Hopton, near Yarmouth, on January 1st, 1902, and passed into the collection of the late J. B. Nichols, father of my friend, J. C. M. Nichols, himself a mine of information on Broadland birds, who presented the greater part of his remarkable collection to Charterhouse School, giving the remainder to myself.

Coots, moorhens and water-rails are the everyday familiars of every broad, but the land-rail or corncrake is, alas, nowadays a comparative rarity. I shot one on a fen adjoining Calthorpe Broad in the autumn of 1945, whilst walking up snipe.

Among birds of prey the golden eagle passes up the coast on migration occasionally, the peregrine falcon is a regular winter migrant and the marsh harrier and Montagu's harrier (54), once on the verge of extinction, are now fairly common breeding species at Hickling and Horsey, where they are strictly protected. Goshawks have been recorded from Filby, Acle, Catfield and elsewhere. The kite, once common in the City of Norwich, is now a rarity. The last recorded one was killed at Winterton in October 1881. White-tailed eagles, or sea-eagles, once common on Horsey Warren, turn up at infrequent intervals in winter, but the osprey, fortunately, is a fairly frequent autumn and winter visitor. One was fishing for weeks on end on Hickling Broad and Horsey Mere in 1947. He roosted at night on an oak tree in the reed-girt plantation on Waggon Hill on the edge of the broad. At about the same time another one frequented Fritton Lake for some weeks. Lord Somerleyton gave strict instructions that it was not to be harmed or disturbed.

Hen-harriers are a comparatively scarce winter visitor, but I have seen them on more than one occasion beating low over the fen like setters. The red-footed falcon has turned up on a number of occasions. One was at Hickling in June 1922. No less than three were shot by Mr. Heath of Ludham Hall at Horning in 1830. The merlin is a regular autumn and winter migrant, whilst the kestrel and sparrow-hawk are always with us. Honey buzzards are passage migrants, sometimes in fair numbers, whilst the common buzzard also turns up in spring and autumn in small numbers.

In Sir Thomas Browne's time, the white stork was a more or less regular migrant. Nowadays, it is occasionally seen on Breydon, where the spoonbill is a regular visitor in April, May and June, sometimes being seen as late as November. In Sir Thomas's time spoonbills bred in the Reedham heronry, and the regularity with which they visit Breydon, Hickling and other places nowadays gives reasonable hope that they may re-establish themselves as a nesting species. Anyone who has seen these incredibly lovely birds nesting in scores on the Dutch fens at Naardemeer and on Texel Island, as I have, can only pray that this ivory beauty will once again add grace and charm to the marshland scene. A flight of spoonbills, seen against the sunset, is one of the loveliest sights on earth.

A hundred years ago that equally beautiful bird, the glossy ibis, was so common in the Norfolk fens that it was known by the marsh-men as the "black curlew" and was frequently shot. Nowadays, it arrives in small parties in spring and autumn. In 1936 four were seen and two were shot between September 11th and October 3rd. A much rarer bird, the black stork, has been recorded three times in

Eastern Norfolk, the last occasion in 1934. There is a good specimen in the Norwich Museum.

The heron is extremely common and heronries exist in Broadland at Horning, Horstead, Hoveton and Mautby, where I have seen them recently nesting in the trees surrounding the decoy, at Reedham, Ranworth, Rollesby, Heigham Sound, Stokesby and in scattered trees around Wheatfen Broad. That charming bird, the purple heron, which gives so much grace to the fenland scene in Holland, is only a rare vagrant, whilst the great white heron is even scarcer. One is recorded as having been picked up near Yarmouth many years ago. A specimen of the buff-backed heron was shot on Breydon Marshes on October 23rd, 1917, and, after being mounted by Saunders of Yarmouth, it was bought by the late J. B. Nichols. The squacco heron has turned up once or twice at Ormesby, at Burlingham, at Surlingham Broad and at Horning, whilst about twenty specimens of the night heron have been recorded. The little bittern, which was seen at Hickling on March 27th, 1929, and at Wroxham on May 10th, 1938, probably occurs oftener than is suspected but, owing to its very small size and skulking habits, it is a most difficult bird to locate and identify. I have two specimens, believed to have been killed on the Broads in the sixties or seventies.

As for the common bittern(49), once rare and now no longer uncommon, these were such an everyday occurrence a hundred years ago that as many as half a dozen were sometimes shot in a day. At home, in the Cambridgeshire fens of Burwell and Wicken, my great-uncle often saw two or three in the course of a day's snipe-shooting. My father shot one there in 1905, after which none were seen for years. On the Broads they had decreased to such an extent that the last nest was said to have been found in 1868 at Upton Broad. After that, they appear to have completely died out as a nesting species, both at Wicken Fen and on the Broads, merely occurring as migrants from Holland.

Luckily, within recent years, this fascinating bird has re-established itself both at Wicken and on the Broads. On my own fen in Cambridgeshire, known as Adventurer's Fen, I always had two or three pairs breeding regularly each year until the place was drained in 1941. To-day, an occasional pair still nests in Wicken Fen, but, fortunately, on the Broads they are becoming an everyday sight again. It seems that they began to re-establish themselves in Broadland in 1900.

Unfortunately there are still people who shoot anything on sight simply because they do not know what it is when it gets up. I have myself seen five bitterns shot "by accident" in the following places: one on the Herringby Hall marshes, on the Bure, in the winter of 1935, when it was mistaken at night flight for a goose; two in 1938 on Adventurer's Fen, when one was mistaken for a pheasant; one on Martham Broad in 1946, when the shooter thought it was a duck; and the fifth on the Waxham Marshes in 1949, when the offender calmly informed me that "he thought it was an owl". The plain fact is that no man should raise his gun against any bird of whose identity he is uncertain. The average shooting man is a good sports-man, a good naturalist and a preserver of rare birds. Indeed, we owe it almost entirely to the efforts of such good sportsmen as the late Lord Lucas, one-time owner of most of the Hickling property; my old friend, Lord Desborough, who succeeded him; Major Anthony Buxton at Horsey Hall; Colonel Henry Cator at Ranworth and Captain Tom Blofield of Hoveton House, that the bittern has been given the protection which has resulted in its becoming once again an established breeding species.

Nothing is more enchanting than to hear that ghostly booming note, the essence of mystery in the silence of a marshland night, when stars glitter in the spring sky, oceans of reeds sigh in the wind and the silence can almost be felt. The bittern is the bird-spirit of these haunting solitudes.

Among smaller birds which are typical of the Broadland scene are the reed bunting, "the reed sparrow" of the marshmen, that graceful and lively little spirit of the reed-beds; the grasshopper warbler, whose reeling song fills the midsummer night from dusk to dawn; the snow bunting, who usually arrives in October, goes in March and somehow typifies the white loneliness of the winter marshes; and the wagtails which flit with electric activity up the dykeside. The marsh titmouse is not uncommon and the rare willow titmouse has been recorded three times, once at Beccles, once at Hickling in 1927 and once on the coast. In winter the continental golden-crested

54   A Montagu's Harrier

55   Sailing on Salhouse Broad

56   The River Ant at Ludham Bridge, Norfolk

wren arrives from the Continent more or less at the same time as the herring shoals appear off the coast, which is why the marshmen call them "herring spinks". They arrive in October, sometimes in big "rushes", and spread all over the Broads. The much rarer fire-crested wren has turned up about seven times.

Most charming of all is the bearded titmouse, that elusive and utterly delightful little bird with a call-note like the tinkling of tiny silver bells. This fairy bird, with its delicately pencilled dark moustaches, long graceful tail and endearing habit of flitting from reed to reed, whilst it follows the passage of a boat, was, towards the end of last century, on the verge of extinction. Gurney was told in 1889 that there were no more than two pairs in the whole area of Hickling and Heigham Sounds. This decrease was due almost entirely to the craze for collecting in the last century. To-day, they have re-established themselves in reasonable numbers, despite the two terribly hard winters of 1916-17 and 1947-8, which killed them off in scores.

The animals of Broadland are, as you might expect, mainly the animals of marsh and water. There may be a lone red stag or a shy and dappled fallow buck stealing like a sunlit shadow, on rare occasions, through the woods that lie within sight of Norwich, but they are park escapes, not of the old feral stock, whose bones and antlers turn up in the peat. Nor are there many foxes. The fox is no lover of too much damp, although he is a deadly enemy of sleeping ducks and, on the Essex coast, will hunt the saltings far out, a mile or more from shore, and judge the turn and flow of the tide to an expert nicety. But somehow he does not seem to flourish amid the coverts and reedland of the Broadland scene. Perhaps that is because there are still gamekeepers who know their job, and this is no hunting country.

But the otter flourishes (53). He is king of the rivers. There are otters on every broad and up every flower-starred dyke. Barton Broad and the shallow reedy wastes of Rockland are strongholds of otters. At Hickling you may see their slides on muddy banks and, when ice has covered the water and snow has fallen on the ice, you may see also where otters at play have pulled another along on his back over the frozen mere. They are kittenish, playful, easily tamed, creatures of infinite grace, more English than the English race itself, but, alas, they eat not only fish, of which heaven knows there are plenty enough, but they kill full-grown wild ducks and even, in sharp winters, go up into the woods and kill pheasants. Otters have been killed on the Broads up to 30 pounds or more in weight. They will always endure so long as reed and water last.

An equally large and interesting mammal which, within the last few years, has become an accepted wild animal is the nutria, or great South American marsh-rat. They are a type of swamp beaver, look like immense rats, are perfectly harmless and run up to 28 pounds or so in weight. They feed on marsh herbage and do a lot of good by chopping down and eating much of the vegetation which threatens to overgrow so many broads and hidden waterways. They will actually clear a quarter of an acre of marsh vegetation in a night. It is a thousand shames that whenever one appears some lout with a gun immediately shoots it. However, in spite of such witless persecu-tion, the nutria, which established itself during the last war as an escape from local fur farms, is increasing in numbers and looks like becoming a permanent and truly wild Broadland animal.

Polecats are now extremely rare in the district, but here and there a few exist, and it is doubtful if they will ever be utterly exterminated. They manage to hold their own, sparsely but doggedly, in the treeless and almost reedless cultivated fens in West Suffolk and Cambridgeshire, near Mildenhall, Littleport, Magdalen Fen and the Isle of Ely, where odd specimens have turned up during the last six years, so there is every reason to expect a few scattered pairs to recur every now and then among the broads. The badger, no marshland animal but a lover of light and sandy soil, occurs occasionally on the higher lands surrounding the district, and it would not surprise me if there is more than one "sett" among the sandy woods and hollow little "lokes" of the Herringfleet Hills.

Stoats, known to every marshman as "lobsters" or "minifers", are common enough, as are weasels, locally called "mouse-hunters".

Hares swarm on the marshes and rabbits abound in the sandhills. Moles are abundant on every marsh and hedgehogs pursue their spiny, midnight ways on the higher and drier land.

Rats, like the plagues of Egypt, are universal and incorrigible, but that loathsome tribe provides the almost unique distinction that, in Yarmouth, you may still find the old English black rat and the even rarer Alexandrine rat, an exotic escape from visiting ships which has somehow established itself with tenuous persistence.

The water-rat, or vole, that charming little miniature beaver, is the beady-eyed, brown and harmless little friend of every holiday-maker who moors his boat by the river bank or pitches his tent beneath a waterside willow. As for field voles, which the marshmen call "rannys", they swarm on every marsh and upland, and when, as periodically happens, there is a plague of them, the short-eared owls who breed on the marshes and wheel by day like buzzards above the spreading levels are reinforced by hordes of their cousins, who flock in across the North Sea from Holland, drawn by the same strange, wild telepathy which causes the snowy owls and eagle owls at Baltic forests to attend in deadly trains upon the periodic plagues of lemmings.

As to seals, porpoises, whales, grampuses and dolphins, these are creatures of the sea, all of which have been recorded from Yarmouth and the coast. A seal has been up-river nearly as far as Norwich, and I know a man who hooked one, to his nightmare fright, on a pike-line in the Yare.

Snakes abound in the marshes, where the grass snake sometimes grows to more than 4 feet in length. The adder, unfortunately, is all too common on some marshes, particularly in the Hickling area, while the harmless blindworm is comparatively often found.

When we come to fish, we are, praise be the shades of Cotton and Walton, who never knew Broadland delights, in a very paradise of coarse fish. There is no better place in all England for monster pike, great fighting perch, slab-sided and lethargic bream, golden and pig-like tench, monumental roach and huge and terrifying eels. Pike have been caught up to near on 40 pounds, whilst eels are taken in the marshmen's eel "setts", not merely in pounds but by hundred-weights and tons. I have told in *Marshland Adventure* something of the mysterious and never-yet-fully-known story of the eel and of the monsters up to 9 pounds in weight which have been taken in these waters. They are a story in themselves and the mystery of their migration and of the way in which the moon and the tide, dark nights and wild wet gales, govern their movements, is fascinating guess-work.

Carp are not common, but there are some in Barton Broad and a few in Hickling and Fritton. The bright and golden rudd is universal and sportsman enough to take a fly, whilst the flashing little dace, who has almost the quality of trout, is common in the Waveney and on sandy patches in the upper waters of the other rivers.

Here and there you will come across a miller's thumb and lots of loach and minnows, on the stony shallows of the upper reaches, whilst those odd fish, lampreys and burbots, occur in the Yare, Bure and Waveney and sometimes in Breydon.

Trout are in the upper waters of the Bure and the Yare and once or twice have been taken at Acle, whilst salmon and salmon trout have occurred rarely but with some persistence.

As for sea-fish, almost every sort is caught either off Yarmouth or has occurred on Breydon, including some extremely rare and exotic species.

The plant life of Broadland and the extraordinary range of its entomology is a subject in itself, of which I have but the sketchiest knowledge. It is enough to say that you will find every lovely marsh-land plant from water-lilies, in an incredible profusion of beauty, to water-mint and willow herb, creamy meadow-sweet and arrowhead, with an incredible diversity of reeds and sedges and tiny water flowers, which cover the levels with a sea of colours and star the waters with beauty.

In its wild loveliness, this land of secret waters and misty levels, of greenish dawns and breath-taking sunsets, is a place where, as my old friend, the late Maurice Baring, that man of enchanted mind, once wrote of an alien land:

It is at dawn that one sees the magic of these waters; at dawn and at sunset that the great broad expanse turning to gold or to silver . . . has a mystery and a majesty of its own. . . .

Once one has known the magic of Broadland, that ancient, mys-terious country of changing lights and marching clouds, of wild geese in the night and curlew whistling in the dawn, of wild duck in the bright air "like a silent singing", of swallow-tail butterflies in imperial glory for a brief day and the running whisper of winds like mice in the reeds, it will linger in the heart and enrich the memory for ever. I think of it as a place where, throughout enchanted years,

> I listened to the strange nocturnal cries . . .
> And straight, as if I stood on dusky shores,
> I saw the tremulous silver of the sea
> Set to some coast beneath the mighty moon.

57 Beccles from across the Waveney

INDEX

The numerals in heavy type refer to the Figure Numbers of the Illustrations